T0059364

THE
POWER
OF
COMMUNION

DESTINY IMAGE BOOKS
BY BENI AND BILL JOHNSON

40 Days to Wholeness: Body, Soul, and Spirit:
A Healthy and Free Devotional

Healthy and Free

The Happy Intercessor

The Joy of Intercession: A 40 Day Encounter
(Happy Intercessor Devotional)

Walking in the Supernatural
(co-authored with Bill Johnson)

BENI JOHNSON

WITH BILL JOHNSON

THE
POWER
OF
COMMUNION

ACCESSING MIRACLES THROUGH THE
BODY & BLOOD OF JESUS

DESTINY IMAGE® PUBLISHERS, INC.
P.O. Box 310, Shippensburg, PA 17257-0310
"Promoting Inspired Lives."

This book and all other Destiny Image and Destiny Image Fiction books are available at Christian bookstores and distributors worldwide.

Cover design by Eileen Rockwell

For more information on foreign distributors, call 717-532-3040.

Reach us on the Internet: www.destinyimage.com.

ISBN 13 International TP: 978-0-7684-4549-7

ISBN 13 eBook: 978-0-7684-4547-3

ISBN 13 HC: 978-0-7684-4546-6

ISBN 13 LP: 978-0-7684-1727-2

For Worldwide Distribution, Printed in the U.S.A.

3 4 5 6 7 8 / 23

Acknowledgments

Many thanks to Pam Spinosi for her continued help with editing. Pam, you are always so gracious and quick to help.

Thanks also to our assistant, Abigail McKoy. You are brilliant. It was fun answering your great questions. Thanks for your help in compiling this book. You made the project fun. Thanks for pulling this out of me and for your writing skills.

I also want to thank Larry Sparks, my publisher. You have been so patient and forgiving with this writing journey.

To Michael Van Tinteren, who labors behind the scenes to make things work—thank you.

And a special thanks to Elizabeth Gan for your help and encouragement.

CONTENTS

Chapter 1

WONDER-WORKING POWER

I was raised in the church. As the saying goes, "I cut my teeth on the wooden pews." My parents were never officially pastors, but they were always leaders in the church. We called them "lay pastors." They weren't licensed, but they helped in the church, mostly with the youth, and were there all of the time. We definitely spent a lot of time in those wooden pews. For us, though, being at church was just a normal part of life. I never resented how often we were there. I loved it. I don't remember ever complaining about going to church. That was where our community was; it was how we did family.

I also loved getting to be a part of what God was doing. I suppose that, even then, I was a people-watcher. When the minister would give the altar call, inviting people to come up front and give their lives to the Lord, I would walk right down and sit on the ground by the first pew. I remember one time, the pastor invited people to come to the front to encounter more of the Lord. I immediately went right down and sat at the end of the first pew. People began to come up, and right away they started to manifest physically. They were crying and rolling around on the ground, encountering the Holy Spirit in new ways. This was many years before the renewal in the '90s, where this kind of activity became a bit more normal. I had no idea what was going on! But I knew it was the Lord. I don't remember being scared at all. Even as child, I loved seeing how encountering God changed people.

Our church, like most churches, had a monthly tradition of taking Communion as a congregation. All those who knew Christ as their Savior celebrated the death and resurrection by sharing in Communion. As a young girl, I thought the best part of this was that I got to eat a little wafer and drink a doll-sized cup of juice. That was pretty fun! At that time, I was getting to participate in the joy and celebration of Communion, but it would be many years before I began to fully experience and understand the power of this tool that Jesus gave us. In fact, it was really only a few years ago, when my husband became so ill that his life appeared to be in jeopardy, that I began to understand Communion in a whole new way.

In First Corinthians 11:23-26, Paul writes:

For I received from the Lord that which I also delivered to you: that the Lord Jesus on the same night in which He was betrayed took bread; and when He had given thanks, He broke it and said, "Take, eat; this is My body which is broken for you; do this in remembrance of Me." In the same manner He also took the cup after supper, saying, "This cup is the new covenant in My blood. This do, as often as you drink it, in remembrance of Me." For as often as you eat this bread and drink this cup, you proclaim the Lord's death till He comes.

In the midst of His betrayal and impending death, Jesus gave us a tool. He gathered His disciples around for the Passover meal, He gave thanks, and then He gave all believers a way to remember the New Covenant that was about to be made on the cross.

I have always taken Communion whenever I have felt prompted by the Holy Spirit. As an intercessor, I have included Communion as a part of my prayer time. It has always been wonderful and powerful. However, it wasn't until Bill got sick several years ago, that I grabbed on to Communion in a more intentional way. Something shifted for me. Since that time of taking Communion daily in the hospital with Bill, I don't wait for Communion Sunday at church or even for the Lord's nudging. I've started to take Communion as a tool in my intercessory toolbox, as a purposeful and proactive part of my relationship with the Lord. I usually take it every day, sometimes multiple times a day, and this new intentionality has shifted my expectation and understanding of the power behind that little wafer and small cup of juice.

A Tool of Intercession

On Sunday, April 9, 2017, our church body ended a corporate fast. My husband preached a wonderful

sermon on the impact of Communion, and at the end of the service we took Communion as a congregation. We prayed together, applied the blood of Jesus to our families and communities, and celebrated what Jesus did for all mankind. That morning, I prayed—like I always did—for each of my family members. But I also felt moved to pray for two of my best friends' children who were lost in their spiritual lives. I pleaded the blood of Jesus over their lives and remembered all that Jesus had done for them when He went to the cross. Even after we were finished taking Communion, though, I couldn't shake the feeling that I was supposed to keep praying for them.

Sometimes the Lord invites us into what I like to call seasons of prayer. These are moments in time when something or someone is put on our heart to pray for, and we just can't let it go. In those seasons, the Holy Spirit will press upon us to keep praying for that specific person or issue. This intense focus may last just a day or much longer. And, in that time of prayer, we may get to see the answer to our prayers or we may just be invited into the process without seeing any specific results. But, either way, we continue to pray because we are being pulled to do so. And usually, just as quickly as the season of prayer comes, it will lift.

Praying for the children of my friends lasted for several days. At the end of that time, I knew that I was released from that season of prayer when these two individuals were lifted from my heart. Not that I didn't still love and pray for them, but they weren't constantly in front of my face. Even though there hasn't been a conclusion to their story yet—these two are both still on their journey back to the Lord—I know that that time of praying for them intentionally and taking Communion, pleading the blood of Jesus over their lives, was fruitful. In these moments, we may not always be able to see the direct results of our prayers, but we can rest assured that another seed was planted.

Any time we are entering a season of prayer for an individual or an issue, we are co-laboring with God. When I use Communion during these seasons of prayer, I joyfully get to do my part in declaring Heaven over their lives. One thing that is important for me to watch out for, though, is allowing a spirit of heaviness to remain on me after I pray. Sometimes, when we get burdened in prayer for someone, the weight of their situation can start to drag us down. I lived this way for many years. Now, I'm really careful about feelings of heaviness. For me, if I start to accept a feeling of heaviness, it will try to take me down a path that leads into depression. I try really hard not to carry it. At the end of every prayer, I make sure that I surrender that person or situation back to the Lord so I'm not carrying it. I will take Communion, plead the blood of Jesus over that person, and then I have to let it go. It's not healthy for me, and when we carry that heaviness, there's also an element of withholding our trust from God. My friends' kids are not aided by my depression. I care deeply about their welfare, but ultimately, He's got them. I just get to be on the winning team.

Judy Franklin has worked for Bill and me for over 20 years. Around ten years ago, she heard a teaching on Communion and felt burdened to pray for her son's salvation. When he was six years old, he had accepted Jesus into his heart, and he had been filled by the Holy Spirit as a young man. But, as an adult, he had fallen away from the Lord. Judy prayed for him constantly. He was taking drugs and also transporting them across the border with Mexico. He was in such bad shape that she felt like he was near death. After Judy heard the teaching, she began to take Communion and declare over her son. She started saying things like, "Jesus, You died for Danny. I'm calling on the power of Your blood to bring him back to You. You sacrificed Your body for my son, and because of that, I call him back from the powers of darkness." Every morning she did this, not knowing if anything was changing.

But, after about six weeks, he came to her, curious about what made her so happy. She told him that her relationship with God was what gave her joy. "I then prophesied who he was in Christ," she said. That Sunday, he joined her at church and went forward for prayer at the end. As he was receiving prayer, he was overcome with the power of Jesus and fell over, receiving immediate deliverance. He stood up a new man, filled with Jesus and free from addiction.

Scripture says that each time we take Communion, we are "*proclaim[ing] the Lord's death until He comes*" (1 Cor. 11:26). When we take the body and blood of Christ, we are reminding ourselves whose we are and what He did for all of us. The commentary in the *Spirit-Filled Life Bible* puts it this way, "Each occasion of partaking is an opportunity to say, proclaim, and confess again, 'I herewith lay hold of all the benefits of Jesus Christ's full redemption for my life—forgiveness, wholeness, strength, health, sufficiency.'"[1] When we use Communion as a tool for intercession, we are not only realigning ourselves with Christ, but we are also proclaiming the reality of Heaven over every area of our lives.

A PROPHETIC ACT

When I take Communion, I take it as a prophetic act, applying it to any situation that is weighing on my heart. A prophetic act is a Holy Spirit-inspired physical action that disrupts the atmosphere. Sometimes, I'll feel as though God wants me to do something tangible to activate something that I'm praying into. During those moments, I simply ask the Holy Spirit, "What should I do about this?" Then, I'll feel prompted to—for example—take my shofar into the prayer house that we have at Bethel or go to a specific place to take Communion. In completing the prophetic act, we are releasing something

into the atmosphere that helps the answer to our prayer to break through.

In Exodus, God had the Israelites kill a lamb and put the blood over their doors, signaling to the Spirit of God to pass by without harming the family inside. Moses instructed the Israelites:

You shall take a bunch of hyssop and dip it in the blood which is in the basin, and apply some of the blood that is in the basin to the lintel and the two doorposts; and no one of you shall go outside the door of his house until morning (Exodus 12:22 NASB).

The physical lamb's blood didn't save them; the will of God saved them. But the families that participated in this prophetic act were revealing a heart submitted to God. The lamb's blood was a prophetic act that each family did in order to align themselves with God's will and alert the spirit realm as to whom they belonged.

When Jesus led the disciples through Communion, during their Passover meal together, He was creating and modeling a prophetic act that believers could continue implementing. He was giving us a way to align ourselves with Heaven and bring Heaven's reality to earth. Often, when I take Communion, I prophesy to myself. There is something powerful in the spirit realm about the declaration of truth, so I talk to myself out loud. I remind myself who I am, that I'm a daughter of the King and that I'm strong in Him. I pull on the promises of the Bible as they come to mind. I'll say, "I am crucified with Christ" (see Gal. 2:20). I let the reality of the New Covenant wash over me, changing any mindset within me that needs to be changed. I declare over myself, "I have the peace that passes understanding" (see Phil. 4:7). I remind myself that I can walk in His peace no matter what circumstances surround me.

A friend called me one day to tell me that she was going to have a meeting with a top official. As soon as she told me who it was, I began to freak out a little. For several days prior to her phone call, I had felt the push to pray over this official. I prayed for blessings and for the love of Jesus to come. At that point, I was taking Communion three times per day. Each time I prayed and took part in Communion, my main focus had been on this person and her family. There was no way I could have known that God was going to use my friend to speak into this leader's life! But God knew. And He was the one directing my path and my prayer time. As we take Communion, aligning our mind with God's, we are able to partner with Him to see breakthrough. We have the most powerful weapon of prophetic intercession available to us.

A Weapon of Warfare

We are at war. We never want to concentrate on anything the devil is doing. We know he's already been defeated! But, there is a war constantly going on all around us. I share a story in my book, *The Happy Intercessor*, about traveling with a team up to Mt. Shasta. This beautiful mountain, just north of Redding, is considered to be a place of power and worship for many satanic or occult belief systems. So, I thought, *That sounds like the perfect place to bring some godly influence!*

> I felt that we were to go up the mountain and take Communion, pray, and blow the shofar. I had around 150 people as a team that day, so it was a power-charged group, and they were ready to see God. We spent some time walking around the

meadow praying, and then we gathered around the spring and took Communion together. Then I had a friend blow her shofar. After the third blow on the shofar, we all shouted out praise to God. We thought we were the only ones on the mountain that day. We were wrong. As we left the meadow and began to walk out, a few of us walked out the lower trail. As we walked out, we passed a tree, and we could hear someone hissing. All of a sudden, a young man jumped out from under the tree and ran as fast as he could past us and down the meadow. No sooner did this happen then we came upon a lady sitting *lotus style* (meditation form) trying to channel. When they channel, they use a coming noise, like a *shh, shh, shh*, repeating it slowly and softly. One of my friends who was with us had used this practice before she got saved, so she knew what was going on. This lady's air space had been so disrupted by our prayers that she was yelling her *shh*, *shh*, *shh*. My friend looked at me and said, "Well, she won't be getting anywhere today."[2]

We never need to be distracted by the activity of the enemy. But we can be aware of the battle that is going on all around us for our minds, for our authority, for our health, and for our peace. We have the winning hand every time! Every time we take Communion, we remind ourselves that the devil has been defeated. The cross had the final word. But I think everyone has experienced being attacked. I'll share about this more in Chapter 4, but this past year I have dealt with health issues, and there are moments when I've been slammed spiritually. I have had to really lay hold of God's promises of peace. I've always considered myself a peaceful person, but I have had to honestly ask myself, *Do I really believe that I can walk in peace when there are so many things attacking that very thing?*

When I'm taking the bread and the wine in a moment like that, I am in a spiritual battle for my health—spirit, soul, and body. Especially when there's something going on in my world that is threatening my wholeness, it's important for me to take Communion more than once a month. It allows me to continually remind myself who I am, who Jesus is, and what He did. Through Communion,

I am brought back to the realization of reality: His world is my true reality, not this one.

Several months ago, I had a young woman contact me through text, asking if we could talk. She was sick and had been sick for a while. In fact, for over seven months she had taken three different rounds of antibiotics, but was still not getting well, and no one could figure out what was making her so sick. I began to ask her questions. Whenever I pray for people, many times I'll ask them questions so that I can figure out why and how a problem started. It's like a little spiritual detective work that empowers me to pray as effectively and specifically as possible.

In speaking with this young friend, I soon learned that the young man she was dating had previously been married to a woman who was now a practicing witch. Now it made sense. She was being cursed. So I gave her a little homework. I told her that once she got off the phone with me, she was to take Communion and continue to take it every day. While she took Communion, she was to apply the blood of Jesus over her own life and send every curse meant to harm her back to where it came from.

As soon as she got off of the phone, she took Communion and did exactly what I had told her to do. Around midnight, she texted me to say that she was already feeling a little better. She took ahold of the power of the cross, prophesied to her body, and the healing began. By morning, she was completely well. A few days later, she told me that her boyfriend's ex-wife—the very woman who had been cursing her—had come down with the exact same symptoms that she'd been experiencing for the past seven months. Several months later, our young friend texted me to say, "I'm still taking Communion, and I'm doing great."

There's an old hymn I remember singing as a girl, and the words still ring true. "*There is power, power, wonder-working power in the blood of the Lamb. There is power, power, wonder-working power in the precious blood of the Lamb.*"[3] There is enough power in His blood to cancel any curse, to save us from our sins, and to heal our bodies. And that power has not waned in 2,000 years; it is very much alive and well.

NOTES

1.   Commentary in *The Spirit-Filled Life Bible* (Thomas Nelson).

2.   Beni Johnson, *The Happy Intercessor* (Shippensburg, PA: Destiny Image Publishers, Inc., 2009), 94-95.

3.   Lewis E. Jones, "There Is Power in the Blood," 1899.

Chapter 2

THE POWER
OF THE BLOOD

Why is Communion so powerful? We've heard of wonderful testimonies surrounding Communion—people being healed, couples who were dealing with infertility taking Communion every day and getting pregnant, and of people falling out in the middle of taking Communion. They had an encounter with the Lord that was so powerful while they participated in the sacrament that their bodies could no longer stand up. That's more than just a wafer and some grape juice. That's the power of the Living God. To understand more about the power behind this, we need to go back and look at covenant. Communion is the reminder that Jesus Himself gave to us the ultimate covenant. It is the body and the blood of Jesus, shed for us.

Blue Letter Bible tells us that the Hebrew word for covenant, *beriyth*, is rooted in a word that means "to cut" or "to eat."[1] Within the expression "cutting a covenant" itself is the graphic depiction of how a covenant was made. When two individuals were cutting a covenant, the ritual included taking a sacrificial animal and dividing the animal into pieces. The two parties would then walk through the scattered carcass, swearing an oath of allegiance in the midst of a path of blood. Essentially, the two parties were making a public declaration that it would be preferable to be like the dismembered animal beneath their feet than to break this promise.

Each blood covenant was a promise of connection, protection, and provision. Like a marriage covenant, where two people are joined into one, the blood covenant created a bond that superseded all other realities. And this was done through the shedding of blood, a public expression that involved the most intimate aspect of life—the blood flowing through our veins. Blood carries and sustains life. Each blood covenant offered a promise that would enhance life, but it came with the potential cost of life.

LIFE IN THE BLOOD

There are doctors who offer what's called *High Resolution Blood Imaging*. In this practice, they claim to be able to take a drop of someone's blood and study it to determine a fascinating array of that individual's health issues. Using a high-powered microscope, they examine the shape of each blood cell. They look at the way that the cell is interacting with the other cells, and they search out the presence of any parasites in the blood. Some doctors have even talked about being able to see the evidence of early trauma—such as broken bones or childhood diseases—within the blood. That is wild! Whatever your opinion is of this procedure, it confirms that we have only scratched the surface in understanding the importance of the blood that flows through our veins.[2]

Unless you're dealing with health issues or you get injured, your blood is probably not something you think of very often. But our blood is miraculous in all that it accomplishes for our bodies. It truly is the river of life. Blood has three main functions: to provide life, health, and protection. The red blood cells transport oxygen from the lungs to every area of the body. They also disperse nutrients and vitamins to the exact parts of the body where they are needed. Our body's very own Amazon Prime!

The white blood cells, along with lymphocytes, help to build the body's entire immune system. Each cell within the blood has a job to do, helping the body to strengthen itself and fight foreign invaders that could make us sick. Some cells build up the immune system, others help the immune system to know exactly what invaders to target. There are certain cells that remember an invasive organism so that the immune system can respond quicker the next time it encounters that same organism. There are other cells that keep the immune system under control so that it doesn't start attacking the good cells within our bodies. What a glorious army the Lord created within us, sustaining and protecting our bodies with this complex combination of blood cells![3]

When we get a chance to study the intricate way our bodies were created, it gives insight into our walk with the Lord. He is so intentional. So it's no accident that blood plays such an integral role in the Bible. There is life in the blood. It's not just a catchphrase.

CULTURE OF COVENANTS

Throughout history, even in cultures that did not know Jesus, the importance of the blood has been paramount. In the ancient world, a promise that included blood was distinguished as a covenant; it was unlike any other promise you could make. Merriam-Webster defines *covenant* as "a usually formal, solemn, and binding agreement; a written agreement or promise usually under seal between two or more parties especially for the performance of some action."[4] Blood was a crucial part of this contract. By shedding blood, the covenant was an intimate profession of a lifelong promise.

In H. Clay Trumbull's fascinating book, *The Blood Covenant*, he details biblical covenants, but he also examines the tradition throughout the world. One example he finds is that of the Karen people in Burma.

While retelling this account, he explains that the Karens had three levels of truce-making between tribes in that region. The first, and weakest, was eating a meal together, which simply signified that there would be peace for the moment. If the tribes wanted to symbolize a stronger truce, they would plant a tree together. With this truce, peace would exist between the two tribes as long as the tree remained alive. But it was the third kind—the blood covenant—where the true power of the promise was found.

Trumbull explains,

> In this covenant the chief stands as the representative of the tribe...The ceremonies are public and solemn...Blood is drawn from the thigh of each of the covenanting parties, and mingled together. Then each dips his finger into the blood and applies it to his lips...This covenant is of the utmost force. It covers not merely an agreement, of peace, or truce, but also a promise of mutual assistance in peace and in war. It also conveys to the covenanting parties mutual tribal rites. If they are chiefs, the covenant embraces their entire tribes. If one is a

private individual, his immediate family and direct descendants are included in the agreement.[5]

Life is found in the blood, and by mixing their blood together, the individuals were effectively merging their lives together. Even cultures that have no relationship with Jesus understand the value of the covenant and the importance of the blood. Trumbull goes on to explain that normally, tribes were not permitted to travel across one another's territory. To prevent this, they created a kind of organic "No Trespassing" sign by tying long grasses together across a trail. "On reaching such a signal, the usual inquiry in the traveling party is, 'Who is in blood-covenant with this tribe?' If one is found, even among the lowest servants, his covenant covers the party."[6] The promise between two individuals, no matter what their rank, would cover the entirety of their community and give them safe passage through a foreign land.

One covenant would cover and re-identify an entire people group, allowing for their survival. There is an old sheep-farming tradition called lamb grafting. If a ewe (mother sheep) loses her baby to sickness or another

tragedy, she will refuse another orphaned lamb, despite her plaintive cries after her lamb's death. Her baby has a specific scent, and she will reject any baby that's not her own. The farmer, however, can take the skin of her dead baby lamb and drape it over the back of the hungry orphan, covering his old smell with the familiar scent. The ewe, thinking that she is smelling her own baby, will accept the orphaned lamb and the baby will survive. Covenants are a covering for those involved. And no one has made greater covenants with His people throughout history than our God.[7]

The Promise of Abraham

Abram was a wealthy man, but he had no son. What he did have, though, was a wonderful relationship with God. God had spoken throughout Abram's life, and Abram had listened. He had left the land of his family, on God's promise, and had even split away from his nephew, Lot. In a time period when your tribe was your strength and security, Abram's willingness to separate himself and trust the Lord speaks volumes about his relationship with God. Each time Abram had an encounter with

God and was given a promise, he built an altar, a place of remembrance. Abram grew to be an old man, and he had been hearing promises about his descendants for years. But Sarai was still barren.

Abram said, "Oh Lord God, what will You give me, since I am childless, and the heir of my house is Eliezer of Damascus?" And Abram said, "Since You have given no offspring to me, one born in my house is my heir" (Genesis 15:2-3 NASB).

I can imagine him thinking to himself, *Ok, I've had all of these promises about the land my future generations are going to inhabit and how my descendants will number like the sand, but I don't even have one child! Has God been talking about my legacy being left to some distant relative this whole time?*

But God knew what his heart was asking.

Then, behold, the word of the Lord came to him, saying, "This man will not be your heir; but one who will come forth from your own body, he shall be your heir." And He took him outside and said, "Now look

35

toward the heavens, and count the stars, if you are able to count them." And He said to him, "So shall your descendants be." Then he believed in the Lord; and He reckoned it to him as righteousness (Genesis 15:4-6 NASB).

This is the kindness of the Lord. Abram needed reassurance on a promise from God that he had held close to his heart. God didn't turn His back on Abram or rebuke him for not having more faith. Instead, God just spoke to him. And, when Abram believed again, God gave Abram points for righteousness!

After that, Abram pushed for even more reassurance: "*He said, 'O Lord God, how may I know that I will possess it?'*" (Gen. 15:8 NASB). He'd just gotten points for believing God, but Abram needed a little more assurance. In response, God cut a covenant with Abram. He tells him about the future of his descendants, how they would be enslaved, but that they would return to inhabit the land. He instructs Abram to bring the animal sacrifice and cut it up. I love this about the Lord, that He so humbly inhabits human culture. His goal is always connection. There were so many ways He could

have handled Abram's insecurity and even so many ways that he could have reiterated the promise, but God chose to cut a covenant with his friend, Abram, in a way that would speak to Abram's heart.

It's clear that Abram was familiar with blood covenants—in just the previous chapter, he had been warned about his nephew's kidnapping by a few men whom the Bible describes as allies of Abram (see Gen. 14:13). These men had cut a covenant with Abram, so they were under obligation to protect him and his family by reporting the abduction. Abram understood covenants. So I imagine that, when God suggested making a covenant with him, it would have felt very meaningful. When it came time to walk through the cut sacrifice, though, only God passed through. "*It came about when the sun had set, that it was very dark, and behold, there appeared a smoking oven and a flaming torch which passed between these pieces*" (Gen. 15:17 NASB). Normally, both parties involved in the covenant would walk through, but this was a God-initiated promise to Abram. God passed through on His own, putting the weight of the covenant behind His words. Abram would have a child, he would leave a legacy, and God would care for His descendants.

Whether they accessed the fullness of His blessing—by following God's way or not— was their choice, but His part of the promise would stand. Soon after this covenant was cut, Isaac was born, and God changed Abram's name to Abraham.

THE NEW BLOOD COVENANT

Jesus Christ shed His blood to cut a New Covenant with His creation. To forever bridge the divide of sin that had put a chasm between man and God, He initiated a New Covenant that was prophesied by Jeremiah.

"Behold, days are coming" declares the Lord, "when I will make a new covenant with the house of Israel and with the house of Judah...I will put My law within them and on their heart I will write it; and I will be their God, and they shall be My people" (Jeremiah 31:31-33 NASB).

This New Covenant at once echoed and fulfilled the promises made to Abram. Instead of coming to earth as smoke and fire, God sent His Son to come to earth in human flesh to walk with us. Instead of a sacrificial animal, torn into two to signify the covenant, God offered His own Son—the spotless Lamb—whose body would be broken as the greatest sacrifice.

We are Abraham's promise fulfilled. Scripture says that, through our faith, we have become Abraham's descendants—as numerous as the stars in the sky and blessed by the Lord. "*And if you belong to Christ [are in Him Who is Abraham's Seed], then you are Abraham's offspring and [spiritual] heirs according to promise*" (Gal. 3:29 AMPC). We are "*heirs according to promise.*" We are the ones God was telling him about thousands of years ago, the ones that would inherit the promises and blessings of the Lord. We are the ones for whom God is a shield and a great rewarder (see Gen. 15:1). The Lord changed Abram's name to Abraham, the father of a multitude, but He also changed our names:

> *No longer do I call you slaves, for the slave does not know what His master is doing; but I have called you friends, for all things that I have heard from My Father I have made known to you* (John 15:15 NASB).

We have access to God in a way that Abraham, the man who was called the friend of God, had only dreamed about.

After Jesus' blood was spilled for the New Covenant, we became not only heirs of Abraham, but also co-heirs with Christ. We share in the inheritance of Jesus.

So then let no one boast in men. For all things belong to you, whether Paul or Apollos or Cephas or the world or life or death or things present or things to come; all things belong to you, and you belong to Christ; and Christ belongs to God (1 Corinthians 3:21-23 NASB).

What Jesus did for all of mankind on the cross was unconditional. He will never go back or change His mind. Accessing the fullness of the blessing of this covenant, though, is our choice entirely.

When we take Communion, we are reminding ourselves of His sacrifice and the personal, unprecedented ways this New Covenant affects every area of our lives. *"...He took the cup after they had eaten, saying, "This cup which is poured out for you is the new covenant in My*

blood" (Luke 22:20 NASB). The blood that was shed was a covenant promise for all of eternity. Nothing would be the same. The blood of Jesus paid for everything. It washed us white as snow, so we could enter the presence of the Lord without an intermediary and without fear. The blood of Jesus gave us freedom and authority. Hell has been defeated for all eternity. And now we get to boldly release Heaven on earth.

THE DEVIL'S PULPIT

Henry Gruver, a powerful intercessor, shares a story of a trip he made into Wales to pray and release the Kingdom. The Lord had directed him to pray over several different high places, including a spot called, "The Devil's Pulpit." Devil's Pulpit was actually a rock slab that jutted out of a large and beautiful mountain. Henry climbed up the mountain to pray.

> When I first came to that place known as the Devil's Pulpit, I stood in that naturally carved stone overlooking the valley and town below, and started reading the Word of God aloud over it. I read about the crucifixion of the Lord Jesus Christ, and then

I began praising God and rejoicing. I took dominion over the devil there, with the intention of taking back that area. I didn't like the idea of any place being called the Devil's Pulpit. The devil shouldn't have a public place from which to preach.

Thinking that he was done with his assignment from the Lord, Henry started to make his way down the mountain. But the Holy Spirit stopped him and told him to go back up. He obeyed, not knowing why, but he described a powerful peace blanketing him. Henry climbed up higher on the mountain and, suddenly, he found himself looking down into a natural amphitheater surrounded by a dense bank of trees. As he began to explore the area, he started to feel the darkness of the place and understand that his assignment there was not yet done. "Then the winds began to whip up around and about me, and as I watched, what had been a beautiful, calm, peaceful May morning, was now being overtaken by a great storm and howling winds." Henry felt the eeriness of the moment, as the winds thrashed the giant trees around him.

He made his way down the amphitheater to the bottom where, in the center of the depression, there was a stone altar standing in the middle of a circle of charred and blackened dirt. On top of the charcoal, slate slabs had been laid. "Now remember, people in the occult like to walk over hot coals. They walk through the fire because it gives them faith, they say, to have stronger belief in their god. That is a satanic counterfeit of God's word, which says we can walk through the fire and not be burned (Isaiah 43:2)." As Henry began to realize what this location had been used for, he stepped onto the slate slabs. There were no flames underneath them, but "as I began to walk on those slate stones, my feet actually became as hot as fire. I reached down and held my hand just above the slate, and didn't feel any heat at all...I thought, 'Lord, what do you want me to do here?'"

Henry felt like the Lord told him to start making declarations over the land. "When we are remitting sins, and claiming back the land, God wants His Word spoken over that land." The devil had used this ground for long enough. It was time to reclaim the entire mountaintop for Kingdom purposes. As he walked throughout the amphitheater, he declared the sovereignty of the Lord over that land and began remitting the sins of all who had come there for satanic purposes. Henry felt like the

Lord asked him to climb up on the altar to speak His words out over the land.

> As the wind was howling through the trees, I stood on that big stone altar and cried out, turning and facing the north, the south, the east, and the west. The declaration took form as I opened my mouth, and let it be known that from this time forth things would be different. Anyone entering this area intending to commit any act, deed or gesture to Lucifer—the god of this world—would come face to face with the power of the shed blood of Jesus Christ and the power of the Holy Spirit.

It wasn't until several years later that Henry received confirmation of what he had experienced in the spirit up on the mountaintop. He was introduced to a satanist high priest, and while the man was grilling him about why he would walk and pray over the land, recognizing the spirit in the man, Henry told him the story of The Devil's Pulpit. Suddenly, the man's countenance changed. He couldn't believe that Henry had been allowed in that place. It wasn't until Henry described every detail of the amphitheater—down to the color of paint on the stones—that the priest believed him. "'So, you're the one! You're the one! You're dangerous!' It was my turn to interrupt him, 'No, Stop right there. I'm not the one; and I'm not dangerous. I stay under the covering of the blood of the Lord Jesus Christ. He's the One Who is dangerous to you.'" With a renewed concern, the man asked for Henry to take a map and point out all of the mountains in Wales where he had been praying. Suddenly, it hit the priest. Shaking, he said, "'You took out all our high places, all over this country. Every year we were losing high places and we didn't know who was doing it.'"[8]

FOREVER CHANGED BY HIS BLOOD

Once, I went out to my son's property to walk and take Communion. They live out on 15 acres, so it's a peaceful place to think and pray. While I was meditating on Communion and all that Jesus went through on the cross, a thought popped into my head: "Every time you take Communion, you remind the devil of his failure." There is power in the victorious blood of Jesus. That power was not just for the salvation of our souls at

Calvary; that power is for right now. Romans says that "*the Spirit of life in Christ Jesus has set you free from the law of sin and of death*" (Rom. 8:2 NASB). The blood of Jesus wiped out the power of sin and the judgment that leads to death. Forever. God took back dominion over the earth and kicked out everything that was once ruled by darkness. As heirs with Christ, we have that same authority through Jesus. And when I take Communion, I am not only aligning myself back up with my true identity as a daughter of God, I am also reminding the devil that he lost. The devil has to watch as I celebrate the resurrection power of Jesus.

The New Covenant has been cut, once and forever. Never again would we have to slice a cow on a hill to walk through it as a sacrifice. Never again would the priest have to go into the Holy of Holies, not sure if he would come out alive, in order to rectify the sins of the people for another year. There was a shift in the atmosphere with the death and resurrection of Jesus Christ. It changed everything forever. We take his blood, represented in the wine, as a beautiful memorial of what Jesus did. By His blood, we can be saved, healed, and delivered.

NOTES

1. *Blue Letter Bible,* s.v. "beriyth," https://www
    .blueletterbible.org/lang/lexicon/lexicon.
    cfm?Strongs=H1285&t=KJV.

2. "The Hilu Institute Clinic Visit Summary,"
    Foundation for Alternative and Integrative
    Medicine, accessed November 14, 2018, https://
    www.faim.org/the-hilu-institute.

3. Carl Bianco, "How Blood Works," HowStuffWorks,
    April 01, 2000, https://health.howstuffworks.com/
    human-body/systems/circulatory/blood.htm.

4. *Merriam-Webster,* s.v. "covenant," https://www
    .merriam-webster.com/dictionary/covenant.

5. H. Clay Trumball, *The Blood Covenant: A Primitive
    Rite and Its Bearing on Scripture* (New York: C.
    Scribner's Sons, 1885), 313-314.

6. Ibid., 315.

7. A. Richard Cobb, "Grafting: A Lamb Saving
    Management Tool," Sheep & Goats, November 7,
    2007, http://livestocktrail.illinois.edu/sheepnet/
    paperDisplay.cfm?ContentID=9831.

8. Henry and Judith Gruver, *Cross-Wise, A Prayer Walker's Manual* (Woodbine, IA: Joyful Sound Ministries, Inc., 2006), http://www.pdxprays.com/uploads/3/9/1/6/39160377/prayer_walking_handbook_-_henry_gruver.pdf.

Chapter 3

SOZO FOR ALL MANKIND

In 2015, Bill started getting sick. For months, he had trouble eating and keeping food down. He would have a bad spell, and then his symptoms would seem to disappear for a little while. But then he'd get sick again. He tried changing his diet and getting medical advice, but it wasn't getting better. Finally, in the spring of 2016, while he was teaching in Europe, he became very ill. After speaking one evening, he went back to his hotel room and threw up 20 times. He was able to fly home and, once he got back, we knew we needed some serious help.

We went to our local doctors in Redding, but they said, "We're not touching this one." They sent us to a specialist in San Francisco instead. By this time, Bill wasn't able to eat or drink anything. The hospital put him on an IV to keep him hydrated, and they ran a barrage of tests. Finally, they discovered that there was a growth in his small intestine that was almost completely blocking the passageway. His body was filling up with fluid. The medical staff prepared for surgery to remove the growth, not knowing how invasive of a procedure they would have to do.

Before we went down to San Francisco, before we knew there was a growth, we had begun to take Communion every day at home. We would take the elements, give thanks, and proclaim all that Jesus did on the cross. We would remind ourselves and the enemy that divine health is our birthright. We would declare, "This is Your body, broken for us. This is Your blood that was poured out for us. You died for our sins as well as our sicknesses. We align ourselves—spirit, soul, and body—with all that You did." Bill felt sick, but we were fighting it. And our weapon was Communion.

Once he was in the hospital in San Francisco, he wasn't able to take Communion anymore. He couldn't eat or drink anything at that point. That's when it became serious. We had to beat this thing. Sickness was not going to win. So we said, "The circumstances don't matter; this hospital bed doesn't change a thing. We believe that God is our healer, and we're aligning ourselves with that every single day." So I began to take Communion for him. We would pray together. I would take the elements for myself and for Bill. It was an incredibly sweet time of God's presence. We had so much peace through the whole journey.

As the surgery day drew near, the doctors told us that, unless the mass moved one centimeter away from where it was positioned, they would need to perform a very serious, life-altering procedure. Hearing that, I immediately got the word out to family, friends, and intercessors, asking them to pray and take Communion for this shift. We needed that growth to move! The day of the procedure came, and the whole family waited, praying, to hear the news. When the surgeons were done, they gave us the update—the growth had shifted just enough. They were able to perform a procedure that was much less invasive with a quicker healing time. What could have been a scary day became a day of celebration. The whole family was cheering when we got that news. We knew that God had done a miracle.

SOZO HEALING

Jesus died for our sins and for our sicknesses—anything that threatens to steal, kill, or destroy our life in Him is not of Him. When He went to the cross, He carried with Him every dark thing of the enemy and was the eternal sacrifice on our behalf. Isaiah 53:4-5 says:

> *Surely He has borne our griefs*
> *And carried our sorrows;*
> *Yet we esteemed Him stricken,*
> *Smitten by God, and afflicted.*
> *But He was wounded for our transgressions,*
> *He was bruised for our iniquities;*
> *The chastisement for our peace was upon Him,*
> *And by His stripes we are healed.*

This passage of Scripture prophesies the crucifixion and the only moment that God had to turn His face from Jesus. When Jesus took the weight of sin upon Himself, there was no way for God to be a part of that. Can you imagine the sorrow that Christ would have experienced? He had known what it was like to live in total union with the Father. I imagine that it would have been crushing for Him to be without God's presence.

Isaiah 53 verse 3, directly prior to the passage above, describes Jesus' rejection by humanity, saying that He was "*A Man of sorrows and acquainted with grief.*" That word *grief* is the Hebrew word *choliy*, meaning sickness, disease or sadness. It comes from a root word that literally means "to be worn down."[1] Jesus carried all of our sorrows, our anxieties, our illnesses to the cross and died. He took the *choliy* of the world onto His shoulders so that we could be *sozo*—healed in spirit, soul, and body.

When Bill and I were in the hospital taking Communion together in remembrance of all that Jesus had done, healing was a part of that. We knew that healing was ours because of the cross, and we applied it through Communion. I know that there are some who believe that God no longer heals, that all miracles ended with the apostles. This is such a sad thought to me. Jesus endured the unimaginable on the cross in order that we could access salvation and wholeness. We deny the power of the cross when we deny the power of God healing today.

I remember while traveling, years ago, Bill and I were in a coffee shop having something to drink. We noticed a gentleman sitting at the table next to us. He had his Bible open with paper and handwritten notes scattered all around him. He looked like he was in deep study mode. We struck up a conversation with him and very quickly discovered that he was a cessationist. He did not believe that speaking in tongues, prophecy, or healing was for today. We had an interesting discussion with him, and I walked away from that experience with one thought— no one can deny your testimony. When I started sharing what God had done in my life, the gentleman didn't have anything to say. People can argue with theology, but your testimony is your most powerful tool.

When we take Communion, remembering what Jesus accomplished on the cross, we are repeating the ultimate testimony again and again. Jesus Christ died so that we could be free of sin, sickness, and sorrow. He is the Healer, and He wants to do it again. Today. Communion has been underutilized far too often. It is a powerful tool, not only for intercession, but also for healing. Take Communion, take it often, and apply the healing power of Jesus to your bodies!

HEALING POWER

Every Saturday morning, we host the Healing Rooms at Bethel. People come for prayer for all sorts of physical, emotional, or spiritual ailments. The first place they go, after they arrive, is into our large sanctuary that is transformed into an encounter room. There, they can worship, sit quietly, or walk around while intercessory dancers, artists, and musicians fill the atmosphere with hope and expectancy. There is such a sweet presence of God there. Because they know the healing power of Communion, the team leading this encounter room offers our guests the opportunity to take the elements. One woman, who drove up from San Diego, was receiving prayer and taking Communion. She hadn't been able to smell anything for seven years.

But while she was lifting the cup to her mouth to drink, suddenly she smelled the juice in the Communion cup. She described feeling as if something had been lifted from her nose!

When we take Communion and declare total health over our bodies, we are aligning ourselves up with what the body of Christ did for us. If we believe what the Bible says, that "*by His stripes we are healed*" (Isa. 53:5), then there has to be something important in the act of partaking in His body during Communion. His body suffered so that our bodies wouldn't have to. When we take the bread, we are testifying that He is the healer, that we don't have to walk in sickness, that what Jesus did on the cross changed everything.

Elizabeth Lawson, a member of our Bethel community, had dealt with a seizure disorder for 30 years that kept her on a daily regimen of medication. One of her friends suggested that she begin taking Communion, using her medication, declaring healing over her body. The medication controlled the seizures, so to test out her healing, she would have to take herself off of the pills. She had attempted this many times in the past, working

with her doctors to try to taper down the medication in order to see if she was healed. Within three days of weaning off of the medication, she would experience a very intense grand mal seizure. After 30 years of experiencing this, she explained that she had simply resigned herself to being on medication.

However, in the spring of 2013, she began to experience a renewed hope in supernatural healing. At her friend's suggestion, she began to take Communion every night, using her medication and water. She would take the pills in her hand and, out loud, thank Jesus for His death on the cross for her. She would say, "I eat your body, Lord." Then, taking the glass of water in her hand, she would say, "And I drink Your blood, Jesus."

Elizabeth loved her daily moment of connecting with the Lord over Communion, but nothing changed right away. Six months later, though, she forgot to take her medication one night. That was highly unusual for her, but the next morning she felt the Holy Spirit say, "It's time." She felt prompted to stop her medication. Without the usual month-long process of tapering down, she stopped her medicine cold turkey. Going from three pills per night for over 30 years to none would, usually, have been enough on its own to send her body into seizures. But God. This time was different. Elizabeth experienced no withdrawal symptoms and zero seizures. She was completely healed. At the end of her testimony, Elizabeth wrote, "Oh, and I have a new habit. I celebrate Communion every night. I just don't need meds or water to do it now!"

THE BREAD OF LIFE

John recounts that Jesus, speaking with the disciples, said, *"I am the bread of life; he who comes to Me will not hunger, and he who believes in Me will never thirst"* (John 6:35 NASB). When Jesus gives the disciples this imagery as a way for them to think about Him, He does something that He does often throughout the Gospels. He is taking a natural reality that they would be very familiar with and using that to explain a Kingdom truth. Our food pyramid has undergone some dramatic shifts recently, but for many cultures bread is a staple food in the normal diet. Jesus had come from the throne room of Heaven. He is the King of all kings. But He doesn't say,

"I am the caviar at your dinner party" or "I am the filet mignon of your life," or even "I am like mint chocolate chip ice cream!"

Instead, He says, "*I am the bread of life.*" Bread would have been foundational to the culture at the time. By equating Himself to bread, Jesus relates Himself to something familiar, but not trivial. Bread was intertwined with daily survival. Earlier in that same chapter, Jesus had fed 5,000 from a few loaves and fishes. The disciples had just witnessed the value of bread for the survival of a whole crowd. Bread is life-sustaining. Of the 44 nutrients and vitamins necessary for human life found in food, bread made from freshly ground grain has 40.[2] Unfortunately for all of us, mint chocolate chip ice cream doesn't hold the same nutritional value. When Jesus shares a meal with His disciples on that last Passover, He again offers Himself to His disciples as bread. Jesus breaks the bread, saying, "...*this is My body*" (Mark 14:22). He offers us the chance to align our bodies with His body, broken and resurrected for us. He is our "*bread of life.*" Our survival depends on Jesus. He is life, hope, and healing.

Sid Roth had Dr. John Miller, a chiropractor who has studied Communion for over 20 years, as a guest on his show recently. According to Dr. Miller,

> I took Communion all my life and never once thought about it in connection with healing.... As I meditated on the symbolism of the broken bread, His body, I thought about the 39 stripes He received when He was scourged. He had literally taken the beating due us for our sin. I realized that discerning the body of the Lord meant our focus should be on the Lord. He had already paid the price for our healing by the scourging He experienced, and that we do not have to be sick![3]

Once he made this connection, Dr. Miller started to see miracles happen through Communion. He suffered from chronic headaches, so he began to take Communion daily. "Every day I took a large hunk of bread and chewed it bite-by-bite, meditating on the mystery of exchanging my sickness with Jesus' wholeness, because all my diseases were placed on Him. He paid the price for my wholeness."

He had a friend who had gone through a very bad car accident that had left him without his peripheral vision. "One night when he was visiting at my house, I explained the healing power of Communion to him. It was late at night, about two o'clock in the morning, when we decided to break bread together. As he meditated on the truth of healing through the wounds of Jesus, the lamb of God, his peripheral vision came back."

On another occasion, Dr. Miller had a patient who had the Epstein-Barr virus. It had destroyed nearly 40 percent of her liver, and she was dying. According to Dr. Miller, "she began taking Communion three times a day, discerning the Lord's body, broken for her healing. A year later, she was in perfect health, with no trace of the virus in her blood." Dr. Miller also told a story of a pastor from Florida who had been diagnosed with cancer of the kidney. While he was hospitalized, his mother felt like the Lord told her to take Communion to the hospital. So, she brought bread and wine into his room. As soon as he took Communion, the cancer began to disappear from his body.[4]

I never mean to imply that Communion is some sort of golden ticket. Our relationship with God is not transactional, it is relational. Always. Through these testimonies, my desire is that you would see the power of remembering what He's done for us, of proclaiming who He is to us, and of aligning ourselves—spirit, soul, and body—with His presence. Communion is not just a nice tradition. It represents the body and blood of Jesus Christ. We have access to the transformative power and grace of our Savior. Communion is a powerful tool at our disposal.

NANCY'S STORY

My friend, Nancy, was wedding dress shopping with her daughter, Lauren, last year. It was a happy, exciting occasion as Lauren tried on dresses and chose the gown for her special day. As they left the shop, Nancy's right arm went numb. Confused, she began trying to make a fist to bring back blood flow into her arm. The numbness only lasted a few minutes, though, so she wasn't concerned and they went off to a celebratory lunch. She didn't recognize that she was experiencing the symptoms of a stroke.

The next day, however, her symptoms were much more severe, and she couldn't ignore them any longer. Nancy was taken to the hospital by ambulance and was met there by a group of friends who prayed over her and led her in Communion. The doctors began running all sorts of tests and, one after another, returned to Nancy's room with increasingly bad news. She had had two strokes. She would need to be admitted to the Neurology Intensive Care Unit as they determined the damage they had caused. Searching for the cause of the strokes, the doctors had discovered two blood clots. While they were studying that, they discovered a tumor on her heart. Nancy says, "I remember looking at the doctor as if he was a poor, lost man in the wrong room, giving updates to the wrong patient. How could it be true that I had just sustained two strokes, have two blood clots and now a tumor on my heart when I felt fine? I kept asking him if he was positive he had the right patient."

While the doctors debated the risk of surgery to address the tumor, the neurologist found a tear in an artery in Nancy's brain that had happened during one of the strokes. Soon, she was having intermittent but total blindness due to the brain bleed.

I had to use every discipline I knew to not go down that road of panic.... The bad news continued. My [medical] team soon reported that I had diabetes. My pancreas was not producing sufficiently, so they started me on insulin injections throughout the day. Further tests showed that there were serious changes in my kidney function. With the tumor putting pressure on the heart valve, I could not pass the stress test and there was blockage that would require triple bypass surgery. If that were not enough, I was diagnosed with a rare and incurable blood disorder which required me to be quarantined. Isolation was immediate, but I still had access to my phone to text friends and family asking for prayer support!

I sent a text to Bill and Beni Johnson from Bethel in Redding, CA. "Can you please pray? I need a miracle! I just had two strokes. And they found a tumor on my heart. I was scheduled for surgery, but apparently, I have a blood disorder that presents a clotting issue even with blood thinners. I didn't pass the stress test due to pressure on the heart from the tumor. I cannot live without the surgery but the risk of another stroke or a heart attack is very high during surgery. It's all very surreal because I am not in any pain and feel absolutely normal. Fortunately, Jesus assures me that I will live, even if I die. Great words right now! The hope of the Gospel has never been more real. The sting of death is gone. I appreciate prayer."

What would you say if you received a text like that?

Soon, I got a message back: "OK praying for restoration of your whole body and a miracle. Take Communion for this. Jesus died to heal us too!!!"

I thought, "Whaaaaaaat?!? What does Communion have to do with what I want prayer for? Didn't they read my text? Come on now. Please, say some super spiritual prayer. Or give me a prophecy. Command an evil spirit to leave me

alone. Break generational curses. Or at least quote a verse. But tell me to take Communion? What is that all about?"

I certainly didn't understand, and I wasn't particularly happy with the response. What help could some grape juice and a cracker do? But hey, I was desperate! I apologized to the Lord that I was clueless about this subject. I asked Him to honor my obedience anyway. And so, I began. Blindly following the suggestion, with zero or very little emotion, I daily took bread and juice, while remembering the Lord's sacrifice for me. As the surgery approached, I was living with a confidence that my destiny had been sealed 40 years ago when I first placed my trust in the finished work of the cross.

When the surgery was over, Nancy was in a lot of pain, but the doctors reported that the tumor was benign. But, in the midst of her celebrating, they diagnosed her with Castleman's Disease. There were two options for this disease—if she was carrying the first type, her life expectancy was three to five years.

I was tempted to give in to fear each night, knowing that I still had a high risk of heart attack or stroke in my sleep. I knew this was a real possibility. However, I continued the prescription of daily Communion.... Surprisingly, one by one, the various diagnoses began to fall to the wayside! The Castleman's pathology was not the fatal type, and it was completely removed. Although I had a third stroke, I have zero neurological deficits from any of the strokes! My vision has been 100% restored. The blood clots are gone and have not returned. My blood tests and the "incurable disease" are showing no abnormalities. The tear in the artery is no need for concern, per my doctor. The kidney function is normal and my pancreas only needs a small dose of insulin to maintain normal blood sugar levels while it heals completely. (Testimony yet untold). This is what I know: The Lord loves us and honors the intentions of the heart even when we don't understand everything. Any one of those diagnoses could have snuffed my life short. Instead, only a few months later, I am walking three miles a day without strain, and I am healthy again. I was recently released from the neurologist with his comment, "It's all behind you now. Go enjoy your life." Thank God for the ability to do just that.

We get to come to the Lord with our *choliy*—our grief, our sickness, our pain—and make an exchange. Because of all that Christ did on the cross, we now have access to the same health and wholeness that is found in Him. Our God is the healer. It's not something that He chooses to do or not do; it is who He is. When you take Communion, align yourself up with this reality. Plead the blood of Jesus over your soul, your spirit, and your body. And receive His transformative, healing presence into every area of your life.

NOTES

1. *Blue Letter Bible,* s.v. "choliy," https://www
   .blueletterbible.org/lang/lexicon/lexicon
   .cfm?Strongs=H2483&t=KJV.

2. Sue Becker, "Exposing the Deception of
   Enrichment," (July 16, 2010), https://www
   .breadbeckers.com/blog/deception-of-enrichment/.

3. Sid Roth, "Healing Through Communion," (March
   6, 2006), https://sidroth.org/articles/healing
   -through-Communion/.

4. Ibid.

Chapter 4

CONQUERING THROUGH PEACE

On February 21, 2018, my life changed. Earlier that week, I had gone to the doctor for my annual breast thermography, an alternative to the mammogram test. The thermography uses digital infrared imaging to see if there are any "hot spots," an indicator of precancerous cells. The images came back and, while she studied the results, she became concerned with what she was seeing. Obviously, her concern had me concerned, so just to be sure, I decided to go in for a sonogram as well. When those results came back, the doctor decided to do a needle biopsy on an area of my right breast right there in the office. Then I waited. Those three days of waiting for the results to come in were torturous. There's nothing like not knowing to leave you feeling powerless and absolutely dependent on God's Word. Deep inside, I felt like I knew what the doctor was going to tell me, but I began to pray and believe that whatever had grown inside of me would disappear.

Three days later, the doctor called me into his office and told me that there was cancer in my right breast.

But I was a health advocate! I had written an entire book on health and wholeness called *Healthy and Free*. I had lowered my blood pressure through diet and exercise, and I had lost eight dress sizes in the process. I was careful with everything that I put in and on my body. I'd never felt healthier. So, it all felt like some sort of cruel joke to hear the doctors say the "C" word.

I decided to meet with a top surgeon here in Redding. I wanted a second opinion. She sent me to have more testing done and ultimately agreed with the first doctor. I had cancerous tumors growing in my breast. In addition to the scanning for cancer, I also had my DNA tested. There was a history of breast cancer in my family, so I wanted to see if I had a genetic predisposition for the disease. The test showed an anomaly on one of my genes, basically letting me know that there was a chance that this could reoccur. After the first doctor's diagnosis, I had already discussed having surgery to remove the two tumors. But, when I got the results of the DNA back, I decided to have both breasts removed. Even though it was a more invasive surgery, I knew that having a double mastectomy would help me to maintain my peace in the days to come.

Maintaining my peace has always been important for me, but as soon as I had heard the news, it became essential. Every day after the diagnosis, I was bombarded with new information, medical terminology, and decisions that had to be made as soon as possible. My doctors were wonderful, but every aspect of this circumstance felt like it was attempting to steal my peace. I decided right away, though, that I wouldn't move forward without it.

Several years before, a good friend of ours had gone through cancer and beaten it. He wrote a book about his experience called, *Kisses from a Good God*. And I began to experience just that. Even on that very first day, when

I walked out of the doctor's office with "cancer" ringing in my ears, I felt a kiss from the Lord. As I walked out that door, feeling scared and overwhelmed, I asked Jesus, "What do I do?" I heard him say, "Just love Me." A wave of His peace came over me, and I said back to Him, "OK. I can do that." As I drove home on that first day, I just kept hearing Him say, "You're going to be OK." I clung to that promise.

And so, the journey began. Every day was a choice to walk in peace.

I knew the peace that I was looking for because many years before, I had experienced it in Heaven. Let me explain. I was at a retreat with Judy Franklin. I mentioned earlier that Judy has worked for Bill and me for over 20 years, but she is also highly anointed in taking people on heavenly encounters. She leads people in encounters with the Lord in which they get to experience Heaven with Him. It's a powerful gift. At this retreat, Judy was speaking, and at the end of her message, she had us all lie on the floor, and she began to take us on a journey to Heaven. I was lying on the floor, my head underneath a chair, visualizing Jesus. Almost immediately I went into a vision. In it, I saw my two grandmothers who had passed on. One of my grandmothers was a large, German woman with a powerful, open-mouthed laugh. When I saw her in Heaven, that's exactly what she did. My other grandma had been a wonderful, sweet woman who had taught Sunday school for 25 years. She always had little children around her and, when I saw her in Heaven, she looked exactly the same.

It was so special for me to get to see them, but I also realized that I was experiencing something I had never felt before. It took me a while to put my finger on why I felt so different, but suddenly I thought to myself, *Wait, this must be Heaven's peace. I like this.* It's hard to describe, but it was like my mind was quiet for the first time. It was empty of all noise—all of the feelings, worries, and random thoughts that usually are swirling around. It was all gone, and this incredible peace was there instead. As Bill says, once you experience something from Heaven, it's yours forever. I've tried to cultivate that peace—some moments with more success than others—in my life since that moment.

So, during this journey, every time I had to make a decision about my health, I looked for Heaven's peace. I felt peace about having the surgery right away. I wanted those foreign invaders out of my body! When I understood the results of the DNA testing, there was peace in deciding to have a double mastectomy. Don't get me wrong, throughout this journey there were times of tears. There were times when I needed to lean on my husband and just have a good cry. But I knew God was near. And I knew that His plan was to kiss me all the way through this journey.

I began to see those kisses, those little things that God would bring along the way to encourage me, to remind me that He was watching over me and to tell me that He loved me. One of the first kisses was from a family member who had a dream about me. In part of the dream she saw me bending over and picking up my diagnosis. As I picked it up, it turned to a sword in my hand. Rick Warren says, "Anybody can bring good out of good. Only God brings good out of bad." I felt like God was telling me that this journey would be a victorious one, and once this journey was over, I would have a weapon of His faithfulness that I could bring into battle.

A few days later, this same family member brought me a few gifts to encourage me. She included a necklace that had a collection of charms and pendants strung together. One of the charms was a lovely compass. She told me that she didn't know why she had picked the necklace with the compass on it, but it had felt right for me. I loved the thoughtful gift, especially the compass. Compasses had been special to me for a while. They spoke to me in a reassuring way about God's presence in my life.

My birthday is in August, and back around that time I had seen an artist's work on Instagram that really stood out to me. It was a beautiful watercolor with a compass painted in ink over a wash of different colors. I had mentioned how much I liked this piece of art to our daughter, Leah, so she secretly had it made for my birthday. More than six months went by, and after the diagnosis and after I had received the gift of the necklace, Leah received the painting. For a while, she kept forgetting to bring it by to give me.

She surprised me with the beautiful picture and apologized, saying she wasn't sure why it had taken her so long to bring it over. The artist explained that she'd also had a hard time completing the painting. She felt like there was a lot of warfare going on with the completion of the piece, and she didn't understand why. But God knew. When Leah commissioned the artwork, neither of us could have predicted what I would be going through more than half a year later. But it came at the perfect time. As soon as I saw the painting, I knew that this was another kiss from God. He was speaking to me through these gifts from my family. He was telling me that He was my compass. My job was just to stay focused on Him, my True North.

Taking Communion became one of the kisses from God. I had experienced the power of doing this during Bill's journey back to health, and I grabbed ahold of it during this time. Communion became an everyday thing for me. I would take the juice and the bread, remembering all that Jesus did for me. I would hold onto the promise of healing given to me through His death and resurrection. And, along with this tradition of taking Communion and applying our healing, there came over me a great peace and assurance. He was taking care of us, of me. He had already taken care of everything I needed Him to on the cross. I could rest in Him. I knew that if

I kept my peace, there would be victory at every turn, in every decision. Whenever I took Communion, and sometimes it was three times a day, it would help me stay focused on Him. His promises would steady my heart.

When I was much younger, I dealt with crippling self-pity. It used to envelop me and drag me down into a deep depression. At 18 years old, I remember crying out to the Lord. I didn't know how to handle the depth of what I was feeling. I knew it wasn't from God, but I didn't know how to live carrying that kind of heaviness. One day, while in the bathroom, I prayed a desperate prayer to God: "If you don't do something to help me, I don't know what's going to happen to me." Instantly, as I walked out of the bathroom, I was delivered from that spirit. It disappeared and has never returned.

Even though I have been free from self-pity for over 40 years, I dealt with it for so long that I still know what those thoughts feel like. Throughout this health journey, there were times when I could hear self-pity knocking on the doors of my mind. It's a horrible feeling, and I had committed years ago never to fall into it again. I had to consciously choose not to agree with that spirit and instead, focus on the Lord. Communion was an anchor for me. Whenever I was feeling fear or self-pity trying to creep in, my focus had to stay on Jesus. When we take Communion, we are aligning ourselves with God. He suffered in the most extreme ways in order to bring us life and freedom. There's not really room for self-pity when you're focused on that reality.

From the very beginning of my health journey, I had decided that I would not have chemotherapy or radiation. My doctors were encouraging me to have both of those things done, but I had no peace about it. So, I knew that that was not the road I would take. When I told my doctors, they said that they understood. They told me that it was my body and that they accepted my decision. When it came time to choose where I would have the surgery, I already knew what I wanted. I had told Bill many years ago that if I ever needed surgery, I wanted it performed at a surgery facility in our city. This facility was small and quiet, but it had very high ratings for the excellence of their surgery and recovery care. When I went in for the surgery consultation with both of my doctors, they both agreed that the facility I had in mind was a great choice. On top of that, our insurance let me know that my procedure would be covered there.

All of these things may seem small now, but they were huge for me. I'm sure another facility would have done a fine job with my procedure, but that place felt peaceful for me. Each time something worked out like that it felt like another kiss from God. It reminded me that if something was important to me, it was important to Him. He knew what each of these steps meant to me. He's a good Father. He takes care of His kids, not only in our needs but also in our desires.

In the midst of this, I realized that God had prepared me in many ways for this battle. When the Lord told me, 15 years ago, that He wanted me fit for the long haul, it started me on a journey to health that changed my life. Because of these changes I was strong and healthy—spirit, soul, and body. Soon after I got the diagnosis, I received a word from a friend. He saw the word "benefit" and heard, "Beni is fit for the next season." I did feel extremely healthy, but that fact didn't feel like a cruel joke anymore. It felt like preparation. When I went in to get an EKG before my surgery, the doctor who was looking at my heart said, "Whatever you're doing, keep doing it!" God had prepared me for this fight, and He was going to get me through it.

My first surgery took eight hours to complete. I felt good going into it. I had my friends and family all around me, and I knew they would be in the waiting room the whole time. Because I had decided on proceeding with the double mastectomy, the initial part of the surgery would take five and a half hours. The most crucial part of this step, in my mind, was the biopsy of my lymph nodes. We knew immediately that the tumors in my breast were cancerous, but the doctors wanted to make sure those cancerous cells hadn't traveled anywhere else in my body.

A few weeks before the surgery, I was telling a friend about this who had gone through the same procedure years earlier. She told me that she would pray. A few days later, she called to share what God had told her in a dream. I was to "have NO concern over the lymph nodes." This was another kiss from God. Obviously, I had been concerned. When the surgeons told me what they were going to do, that reality stayed in my mind, and I had found myself wondering what the results would be. But, as soon as she shared her dream with me, that was it. That was all I needed to grab onto that peace. That word sustained me until after the surgery. It was a living word for me. Once I was out of surgery, the surgeons came and gave me the news right away: there was no cancer in my lymph nodes.

I experienced another beautiful kiss through God sending me a wonderful, new friend who also happened to be a health coach. She had also overcome stage four cancer through holistic means. Because this was the healing path that I chose as well, I teased her, saying that God had her move to Redding just for me. But, seriously, she had experience in just about everything that I was going through. She knew where to send me for advice and what care providers I should see in order to help bring healing on the natural level. She was my constant help in all things holistic, and her encouragement sustained me all along the way. I am forever indebted to her for her constant prayers and instructions.

On her advice, we both ended up going to an amazing holistic clinic in Spain, The Hilu Institute, run by Dr.

Raymond Hilu. Honestly, it took me a while to find my peace to go there. I didn't want to leave my family to travel halfway around the world for two weeks. The list of holistic treatments was intimidating, and this was a doctor I didn't know. So I just waited. I knew, by this point, that I wasn't going to do anything without peace, so either I wouldn't go or the peace would come. After a few months, my heath coach brought it up again, saying that she would travel with me to Spain. She wanted to undergo another round of treatments for her own care. Soon after, the peace came, and we made the decision to go.

During this entire process, Communion became my frequent morning ritual. It was something that I hung onto through all of the different doctors' reports and decisions that needed to be made. Spending that time with Jesus—recognizing Him and receiving my healing—made all the difference in the world. Some mornings, especially when we were in Spain, I would join with my health coach and we would take Communion together. It was a wonderful time for both of us, committing our lives and our care to Him. I truly believe that this daily alignment was a large part of my healing process.

As I write this, I am walking in health. The doctors' reports continue to be excellent. I will never forget the prayers I received. There were so many people, throughout this journey, who sent me messages, telling me that they were praying and taking Communion for me, people from all over the globe. It's humbling and beautiful to be covered by so many believers. I will always remember this journey, all of my kisses from Heaven, and how Communion continues to play a pivotal role in my health and in my life.

Chapter 5

THE FIGHT TO
REMEMBER

As soon as I wake up, there are a thousand things competing for my attention. Before my feet hit the ground, I can read news from all over the world, find a recipe for dinner, scroll through photos on Instagram, listen to a worship song, and text my friend. And that's all in a matter of minutes! If the mind is a battlefield, then a big part of the current battle is a fight for space. It's a battle for time, for quiet, and for focus. Now, I'm not saying that everyone needs to have hours each day set aside for time with the Lord. That's wonderful if you can do that, but not every season of life is conducive to that kind of time. When I was a young mother, that just wasn't possible. I had to learn how to turn my heart toward Him for a few minutes while doing the dishes or putting the baby to bed. What we can all do, though, is to create a meditative space—a space for remembering—during our time of Communion with God.

There are some days that, because of my schedule, I take Communion quickly. But, most days I love to take the time to meditate on who God is and what He's done. The Lord wants to reveal different aspects of Himself to us, so every time I take Communion, I ask Him, "What does this mean today? What aspect of You do I need to have at the forefront of my mind today in order to keep myself aligned with You?" He is my daily bread. As I connect with Him, I meditate on His goodness and all that He's done. I take the time to remember.

When Jesus walked the disciples through the first Communion, He commanded them to remember. After both breaking the bread and taking the cup of wine, Jesus says, "*Do this in remembrance of me*" (1 Cor. 11:24). God doesn't need to remember; He lives outside of time. Forgetfulness isn't something He deals with. Remembering is for us. We seem to forget something as soon as we turn around. Have you read the Old Testament? Part of me wants to shake my head every time I read of the Israelites forgetting the miraculous way God showed up for them two paragraphs prior, but then I think about my own life and how important remembering Him has been for me.

Memories have a powerful effect on our attitude and outlook. Bill teaches that if you are having a conflict with a friend, you should only share that conflict with someone who has genuine love for that person. Why? You don't want to vent to someone who will encourage division in the relationship. At that moment, you need someone who is able to remind you—in the midst of the pain—what you love about that person and the value of the relationship. You want someone who can help you pull out of any confusion or defensiveness and into the greater reality of love. It's similar in weddings. Other than the joy of celebrating with loved ones, we invite our closest friends and family to witness our wedding because, when things get hard, we need those individuals to remind us who we are and what we've promised. Remembrance is vital for our walk as Christians. It keeps us aligned with the reality of who we are and the covenant that was made for us.

I've had many beautiful moments with the Lord throughout my life, but there are a few that I return to more often than others because of how they reorient my heart. One of these moments is our trip to Nome, Alaska. (I have the full details of the story in *The Happy Intercessor*.)[1] I went with a team of women up to northern Alaska to pray over our nation. It was the very first prophetic prayer act that I did out in the community, so I wasn't entirely sure how it was going to work out, but while we were on the trip, it became obvious that every single aspect—where we prayed, what we prayed, the people we met, the timing of our departure—had been orchestrated by God. The time of prayer was powerful, but seeing His attention to detail and feeling so in sync with Him transformed me. I think back on this moment, and it reminds me not only of His faithfulness, but also how alive I feel when I'm connected to the Lord's heart in intercession. It's what I was made to do. I keep those memories close as powerful reminders to myself.

Throughout the Bible, the Lord speaks to His people about the power of memory. In Deuteronomy, the Israelites are about to enter into the Promised Land. They've wandered the desert for 40 years, being sustained and guided supernaturally the whole way. Almost an entire generation has passed away, and the children of those who fled from Egypt are about to walk into the "*land flowing with milk and honey*" (Deut. 11:9). But first, Moses gives them some instructions from the Lord. In the first verse of Chapter 11, he repeats the commandment, "*You shall therefore love the Lord your God, and always keep His charge, His statues, His ordinances, and His commandments*" (NASB). But then he qualifies this commandment.

Moses says that the people who have seen the miracles of the Lord, the ones who lived through the parting of the Red Sea and the provision of manna, are the ones with the responsibility. "*...I am not speaking with your sons who have not known and who have not seen the discipline of the Lord your God—His greatness, His mighty hand and His outstretched arm, and His signs and His works which He did...*" (Deut. 11:2-3 NASB). Moses is charging the ones who have seen the nature of God firsthand with the commandments to love and obey God. The testimony of their lives carries a responsibility, not only for themselves, but for the future generations.

He continues, telling the Israelites to remember his words: "*You shall teach them to your sons, talking of them when you sit in your house and when you walk along the road and when you lie down and when you rise up*" (Deut. 11:19 NASB). "Do not forget who the Lord is, and who He has been to you," Moses says. Why is this so important? I can imagine Moses trying to get through to them, "Guys, please, no more of this idol business. Remember who God is and whose you are. Tell your children. Talk about it all of the time. Use any memory tool that will help you. Write it on your forehead, if that helps!"

He follows this encouragement by explaining to them why this is so important: "...*so **that** your days and the days of your sons may be multiplied on the land which the Lord swore to your fathers to give them, as long as the heavens remain above the earth*" (Deut. 11:21 NASB, emphasis added). Remembering is the key to inhabiting the Promised Land. The Lord wants to pour out blessings on them. He wants to bring them into "*a land of hills*

and valleys, [that] drinks water from the rain of heaven" (Deut. 11:11). But in order for them to actually possess this land—to receive this blessing—they need to align their minds with His.

When we take Communion "*in remembrance*" of what Jesus did on the cross, we are stewarding the greatest testimony in history. The Israelites escaped Egypt after ten supernatural plagues rained down on their captors. They walked through the Red Sea on dry land. They were led by pillars of cloud and fire. They were fed supernaturally, never got sick, and wore the same clothes for 40 years. Yet they didn't have Jesus. They didn't have the cross or the resurrection. They didn't have a Savior that took away the sins of the world. Matthew 11:11 makes it clear the kind of gift we have received. "*Truly I say to you, among those born of women there has not arisen anyone greater than John the Baptist! Yet the one who is least in the kingdom of heaven is greater than he*" (NASB). John the Baptist knew Jesus as family, followed God faithfully, yet he was never born again. He didn't know life with the resurrected Christ living inside of him. You and I, we get that honor. We have that responsibility.

FAITH MAKES US HUMAN AGAIN

Memory is a powerful tool. It shapes our present by creating expectation for repetition. The brain is literally creating pathways from your thought patterns. Some of the discussion of this began in the New Age movement, but now scientists who study the brain are confirming what the Bible says: What you allow your mind to dwell on shapes your expectations and, ultimately, your perception of the world. The neurons in the brain strengthen and change with our thought patterns. The more you make certain connections, the more likely your brain will make that connection in the future. Some describe it similarly to the way a popular hiking trail gets worn down and widened. For example, if you're used to thinking the world is out to get you, that neuropathway will have a strong connection in your brain. Something might happen to you, and you think, "Well, there it goes again. I knew bad things happen to me."

But, the grace of the Lord always makes room for transformation. You can change these neuropathways by what you set your mind on. As Dr. Stokes, a psychologist, explains, "...as you practice traveling down new pathways, you naturally weaken old pathways. As you think similar thoughts and feel similar feelings, you either create new habits and beliefs or solidify old ones. Eventually, through repetition and feeling intensity, your new habits run on autopilot."[2] So, when Paul writes to the Colossians and advises them, "*Set your mind on the things above, not on the things that are on earth. For you have died and your life is hidden with Christ in God*" (Col. 3:2-3 NASB), it's not just a nice idea. It's actually advice that will change the "hardwiring" of our brains. We are new creations. We know a reality that is greater than any circumstance we can see. We have "*the mind of Christ,*" and God is inviting us to use it. (See 1Cor. 2:16.)

Bill spoke about the power of testimonies recently. At Bethel, sharing testimonies is a big part of our culture. We have a two-hour senior staff meeting each week where we spend 90 percent of the time sharing about what the Lord is doing all over the earth. It's amazing to hear about the miracles. The world is truly getting better all of the time. But when we hear those, we don't just stop with marveling at God's goodness. We also say, "Do it again, God!" As Bill says, the power of the testimony never depreciates. Whenever you revisit a story of God's faithfulness or His divine disruption in your life, you are revisiting a place of divine encounter. Remembering what He's done in your life never loses power. God is the same yesterday, today, and tomorrow. So when you hear of a miracle that has happened in someone else's life, you know that God has just set the legal precedent of what He wants to continue. Testimonies are not just fond memories. They have a lifespan that's eternal. They continually give God praise.

Our son, Eric, has been releasing the power of the testimony lately surrounding some miraculous transformations with young people who have been diagnosed with autism. The initial healing was powerful and such a time of celebration. But what's been amazing to watch is the momentum on the testimony. Since that first healing, Eric has shared the testimony with other audiences close to ten times. Each time he's shared it, there's been another healing dealing with autism. The testimony increases the faith in the room, and the faith in the room grabs ahold of what was paid for 2,000 years ago.

Erwin McManus, the pastor of a church in Los Angeles, recently came to Bethel for our Open Heavens

Conference and preached a powerful sermon. He started by explaining how unfair he thought Hebrews 11:6 was: "*And without faith it is impossible to please God*" (NIV). He asked, "What other aspect of creation is held to this standard?" But then he started to unravel the differences between humans and other creations. And, ultimately, he said, "Faith is what makes us human.... No other species needs hope. Hope is what connects us to the future.... In the same way that bees create hives and ants create colonies, humans create futures....You have the power to create the future, but the moment you lose hope is the moment you're disconnected from the future."

We were designed to impact the world around us. We have been given the charge to represent a good God and infuse every situation with Heaven. We cannot do that, though, without feeding ourselves on all that God has done for us, thereby building our faith and our hope for what is to come.

A beautiful thread weaves between our past, our present, and our future. In our past, we have what God has done—all of the stories of His faithfulness and grace. In our present, we have the command to remember those

testimonies, to build our trust in God and align ourselves with Him. From that place, change will come. "*For whenever you eat this bread and drink this cup, you proclaim the Lord's death until He comes*" (1 Cor. 11:26 NIV). The act of proclaiming is like sharing the testimony. It is releasing the reality of the cross into the world. When you're remembering God and trusting in Him completely, then you are filled with hope for the future of the world around you. We can take Communion in remembrance of all that He has done for the world and for ourselves personally, and we can look toward the future with hope. Matthew 17:20 says, "*...if you have faith the size of a mustard seed, you will say to this mountain, 'Move from here to there,' and it will move; and nothing will be impossible to you*" (NASB). This promise is embedded in the body and blood of Christ.

Remembering the Cost

Often, we don't really want to remember the brutality of what Jesus went through for us. It's gruesome and uncomfortable. But when I remind myself of the details of Christ's death, I find that it keeps my heart in a posture of overwhelming gratitude. It also renews my perspective on whatever challenge I'm going through. For 33 years, Jesus had lived on earth, three of those spent serving in a fruitful, but probably exhausting, time of public ministry. As He neared the end of His life, Jesus wrestled with what He was about to do.

He knelt down and prayed, saying, "Father if it is your will, take this cup away from me; nevertheless not My will, but Yours, be done." Then an angel appeared to Him from Heaven, strengthening Him. And being in agony, He prayed more earnestly. Then His sweat became like great drops of blood falling down to the ground" (Luke 22:41-44).

Jesus was the only one, besides the Father, who was aware of what He was about to go through. The intensity of that anticipation, not only of His own physical death, but also of the agony of being separated from the Father because of the sin of the world, must have been so painful that He literally sweat blood. When He was carrying that reality, the betrayal by Judas and the rejection from His closest disciples must have been an added weight on His heart. When I take Communion, I stop and remember this betrayal. I don't just dwell on the injustice for its own sake, but I do want to remember the cost of what Jesus did so that I can truly value His gift to me. Thinking through all that He went through in the days leading up to His death also paints a picture to me of how to walk through pain. These moments in the life of Jesus are so brutal and yet so beautiful.

Jesus knew that Peter would deny Him, that His disciples would abandon Him, and that Judas was going to betray Him. But He still sat down to a meal with them and shared Communion. "*The Lord Jesus, on the night he was betrayed, took bread, and when he had given thanks, he broke it*" (1Cor. 11:23-24 NIV). There are a few aspects here that teach me so much. He was well aware of the betrayal, yet Jesus still invited Judas to break bread with Him. He gave thanks. Jesus filled His heart with gratitude, despite being aware that He was about to die and the very people He was dying for were betraying Him. I can't imagine the strength that Jesus had to have to walk through that moment the way that He did. Knowing that He was going to be crucified, He gave thanks. In the midst of betrayal, He opened His heart to His disciples.

So, when I'm remembering the betrayal of Jesus, I'm not just focusing on the injustice. I'm focusing on Jesus. I'm reminding myself of the way that He walked through betrayal. If Jesus can do that, then He's offering me a model for how to deal with my own hurts and grievances. He's showing me what His love can overcome.

I remember the day that this point really hit home for me. I was taking Communion with my husband. Over the years, we have experienced a few people who have focused a lot of energy on attacking our lives and ministry. That day, when we were in the middle of praying for our friends and family, Bill started to pray for each of the people who had come against us. He began to pray a blessing over their families, praying for God's grace to be on their lives and for their physical health. I sat there, listening to my husband and felt totally convicted. I remembered what Jesus went through, and something clicked in my spirit. I realized, "Oh my gosh, I can love these people. Despite everything that's going on, I can love them."

Jesus didn't shy away from the suffering involved in His sacrifice. The agony of anticipation He experienced in the Garden of Gethsemane and the betrayal by Jesus' disciples was followed by excruciating physical pain. He was forced to carry a heavy cross for miles while a crowd threw stones at Him and spit in His face. Once the cross was erected, long nails pierced through the tendons in His wrists and the bones in His feet. For three hours, our Jesus suffered the most horrifying pain as He hung on the cross, experiencing the weight of sin and the distance of the Father.

As a part of meditative Communion, I like to remind myself of what He went through on the cross. One day, I was imagining His suffering, and I realized, "He stayed up on that cross!" Jesus was fully God and fully man. He didn't have to do anything He didn't want to do. He could have taken Himself right off of that cross if He'd chosen to, but He stayed. He stayed for me. He stayed for us. That realization brought a whole new wave of gratitude, because I know that I couldn't have done that. I would have been saying, "Sorry, Dad, but I can't handle this!" Instead, He stayed.

There is a weight to remembering the cost that Jesus paid. I never want anyone to cultivate the heaviness that leads to depression. But there is an important humility and gravity that comes when you are remembering *how* His body was broken for us and *how* His blood was poured out for us. When I meditate on His experience, I remember all over again that His blood is sufficient for anything I am going through. Jesus paid the ultimate sacrifice so that I could be free and whole. If something is threatening that, I know it's not of the Lord. I can see what He went through to untangle me forever from sin and sickness.

WHAT'S AT STAKE

Psalm 78, catalogues the faithfulness of God to the Israelites. Unlike most of the psalms, this one reads like a history lesson, but embedded within the narrative is a warning: Do not *"forget the works of God"* (vs. 7).

We will not conceal them from their children,

But tell to the generation to come the praises of the Lord,

And His strength and His wondrous works that He has done.

For He established a testimony in Jacob
And appointed a law in Israel,
Which He commanded our fathers
That they should teach them to their children,
That the generation to come might know, even the
children yet to be born,
That they should put their confidence in God
And not forget the works of God,
But keep His commandments,
And not be like their fathers,
A stubborn and rebellious generation,
A generation that did not prepare its heart
And whose spirit was not faithful to God
(Psalm 78:4-8 NASB).

The psalmist goes on to explain about the "*stubborn and rebellious generation*" (vs. 8), detailing the many times that they had turned from the Lord and just how poorly that worked out for them each time. Through the mistakes of the Israelites, the author gives us a glimpse of what is at stake if we choose not to actively remember. Verse 7 makes the connection between memory, trust and obedience. "*That they should put their confidence in God and not forget the works of God, but keep His commandments*" (NASB). Dwelling on the goodness of God, continually reminding ourselves of His faithfulness and His promises—these are the building blocks of trust. And, when we trust God, aligning ourselves with His commandments comes so much more naturally. Without our keeping Him in the forefront of our minds, that confidence crumbles, and fear takes hold.

I love how the Passion Translation puts it in verse 22, talking about the Israelites who forgot God: "*They turned away from faith and walked away in fear; they failed to trust in his power to help them when he was near.*" There are very real consequences to our forgetting who God is. When His goodness and faithfulness are not fresh in our mind, we can become calloused toward God. We can feel hesitant to trust in His goodness. And that can lead to a heart that has not been cultivating gratitude. We can see the results of that within our own lives and the lives of the Israelites. As soon as they started forgetting, they began to fear, and they put their trust in something else. Later, the same psalm speaks of the Lord's reaction to their unfaithfulness. "*He abandoned the dwelling place at Shiloh...And gave up His strength to captivity and His glory into the hand of the adversary*" (Ps. 78:60-61 NASB). This verse is incredibly sobering. Because of the Israelites' forgetfulness, because they turned from trusting in God completely, He allowed His presence to be removed from their midst. They were no longer recipients of His strength, and they no longer had access to His glory.

We live under the New Covenant. God has promised never to remove His presence from us, but we still have the same choice that the Israelites had. Will we remember and trust in God's love for us, or will we turn to fear and fending for ourselves? The psalmist describes an all-too-familiar heart issue: "*Even when they saw God's marvels, they refused to believe God could care for them*" (Ps. 78:32 TPT). Will He take care of me? Will He provide for me? Was His blood enough for what I'm going through? Each time we take Communion, we are testifying to the enormous, radical love of God. We are reminding ourselves that we had a debt that we could never, ever repay and that we were condemned to death; there was nothing we could do about it.

But God. His love was so extravagant that He sent His Son to die in our place, to suffer indescribable pain so that He could take on the sins of the world. "*For God so loved the world, that He gave His only begotten Son, that whoever believes in Him shall not perish, but have eternal life*" (John 3:16). This was the first verse I learned as a child. It's a powerful one that we can take for granted because it's so familiar. I would encourage you, as you take Communion, to meditate on this verse. Allow your remembrance of Him to take you to a new level of understanding. It was all for love. Love took Him to that cross, and love kept Him there. When you take Communion, experience the invitation to remember the weighty reality of His absolute and perfect love for you.

NOTES

1. Beni Johnson, *The Happy Intercessor* (Shippensburg, PA: Destiny Image Publishers, Inc., 2009).

2. Hillary Stokes Ph.D. and Kim Ward Ph.D, "Neural Plasticity: 4 Steps to Change Your Brain & Habits," (June 21, 2010). http://www.authenticityassociates .com.

Chapter 6

RELEASING
THE POWER OF
COMMUNION

I n 2016, I felt like the Lord asked me to take Communion every day for the 15 days leading up to the presidential elections. So every day at high noon, I would take my little cup and wafer and remember all that Jesus did for us and all that He was doing in our nation. High noon has become an important time for me to pray. When the sun is at its pinnacle in the sky, everything is exposed. I like to think about the light flushing out anything that's been hiding in the dark places. It's a powerful time to intercede for God's light and truth to expose any hidden things.

I was born to pray. When I go up to the high places—a mountaintop or the top of a city building—to pray and worship, I feel as though I'm doing what I was born to do. I'm in my element. I often go with a team of friends to various places to intercede, and in the last few years we've added Communion to the arsenal of tools we use during these times. Too often Communion can get locked into the routine of church culture. There are great, logistical reasons for churches to have Communion once per month. But that doesn't mean we have to limit ourselves to that! Like every other aspect of our walk with God, if we are only experiencing Communion within the four walls of the church, we are missing out on a gift from Jesus.

Communion is a powerful tool of intercession. And because of that, it's applicable in every area of our lives. At the end of 2017, Bethel invited people to prayer walk in their neighborhoods for three months. In that time, people traveled alone or with friends to whatever part of the city they had on their hearts. We offered a list of prayer targets, but those walking were encouraged to pray, take Communion, and declare truth over our city and our nation. One of the ways that we can tap into the transformative power of Communion is by taking it into our communities. I have more stories of specific prayer walks in *The Happy Intercessor*.[1] These walks are a chance for us to take ownership over our land and the atmospheres over our cities.

Anne Kalvestrand, a powerful intercessor at Bethel, shared an example of this kind of geographical ownership. In 2015, students who had gone through our Bethel School of Supernatural Ministry traveled on a ministry trip to Turkey for the 100-year anniversary of the Armenian Holocaust. This genocide was the horrific killing of around 1.5 million Armenians after WWI, which displaced many surviving Armenians from their land. The alumni who were on this trip were all either of Armenian or Turkish descent. Together, they traveled to the location of some of the conflicts, and they poured the Communion elements onto the ground, praying for the trauma of the genocide to leave the land. The Armenian students forgave the Turks and prayed for salvation to come to all of Turkey.

Proclaiming His Death

First Corinthians 11 says that, when we participate in Communion, we are proclaiming the Lord's death. "*For as often as you eat this bread and drink the cup, you proclaim the Lord's death until He comes*" (1 Cor. 11:26). On the surface, that verse sounds like we're just reminding everyone that Jesus died. But it's more than that. That phrase "*you proclaim*" is the Greek word *kataggello*.[2] It's the same word, used throughout the New Testament, that is also translated as "preached." "*And when they arrived in Salamis, they **preached** the word of God in the synagogues of the Jews*" (Acts 13:5, emphasis added). When you take Communion, you're telling the world about the Lord's death. Every time you partake in the body and blood of Jesus Christ, you are preaching the Gospel. How? Communion is most often thought of as a time of quiet reflection, not bold proclamation. Yet that word *kataggello* is undeniably assertive.

Each time you take Communion, you align yourself with the broken body and the shed blood of Christ. You are remembering what He's done for you. But you are also aligning yourself with what happened three days later. When those Turkish and Armenian students stood together and poured out Communion into the war-ravaged soil, they were inviting the reality of the resurrected Christ, the One who is victorious over sin and darkness, into the history of that land. When we are lined up with the reality of Christ—in spirit, soul, and body—we release that reality into the world. We preach the Good News, not just from a pulpit or with our voices; we preach the Good News with who we are. We show the goodness of God with how we handle situations in our businesses and in our families. Every time we take Communion, then, we are reminding ourselves that we are Christians—little Christs. When we remind ourselves who we are, we can reveal to the world who He is.

Mark Mack served as a California Fire Captain for 30 years with the wildlife firefighters. In 2007, he was assigned to a major fire in the San Diego area. That location had burned four years prior, and a firefighter had tragically lost his life. Mark and his team were stationed in the exact same place. With winds gusting up to 90 mph, the threat was extremely high that the fire would begin to spread. Mark, the division supervisor, was tasked with keeping it contained by any means necessary.

As his shift began, it became obvious to Mark that this was not going to be an easy day. One firefighter sustained a burn; another fell down a hillside, fractured his arm and needed a team to rescue him. After that, an engine crew reported to Mark that they were being fired upon. The crew had been clearing houses in the path of the fire, and they had accidentally stumbled across a meth lab. In a different location, another firefighter fell into a canyon and broke his leg. His rescue required a Coast Guard helicopter. In an incident unrelated to the wildfire, a house caught on fire down the road from where they were stationed. An elderly man wandered away from home, leaving his family terrified that he had been caught in the wildfire (he wasn't). Three traffic collisions occurred that required firemen to be present. And, finally, as Mark was flown by helicopter to survey the fire in his designated area, a warning light came on in the cockpit, and the pilot had to make an emergency landing. All of this happened in the midst of the regular operations needed to contain a 100,000-acre wildfire.

Mark said, "Finally, around 8:30 in the evening things slowed down, and I could catch my breath. I was extremely tired, stressed and very ticked off at God for making me go

through all of that. I had the classic 'Why me?' attitude."
He sat on the tailgate of his truck, feeling overwhelmed
and exhausted. Noticing the box of sack lunches that had
been prepared by a local church, Mark reached for a paper
bag, realizing that he hadn't eaten all day.

The very first thing I pulled out was a small piece
of green cardstock. Written in a child's handwriting in black crayon was, "Thanks, Love Allison." I
bowed my head and wept. Then I heard that still,
small voice and He gently said, "Son, you forgot
why you were here. All of these things happened
today because I knew you would handle them.
That's why I put you here. You forgot that it's not
about you...it's about them and you bringing My
love."

I brokenly asked Him, "How did I show them
Your love? It was all crazy and fast and I never even
though about You, truth be told."

He replied, "You were here, where I wanted you to
be." Then the Lord said, "I want you to take Communion here and now, and I want you to remember Me."

Mark reached into his sack lunch and pulled out some Ritz crackers and a bottle of Gatorade. In the middle of a major fire, he took Communion and remembered why he was doing what he was doing. "Ever since that day, whenever I get angry or fearful, I remember. I remember a card written in crayon from a nine-year-old girl. I remember how much He loves me. And I take Communion in remembrance of Him."

Releasing it in Our Businesses

When we remember who He is and who we are, we can offer the world a glimpse of a God they may have never seen before. We can reveal to them a Father who cares, who desires to be intricately involved in every aspect of their lives. Andy Mason, the head of Heaven in Business, has been teaching this principle to people in the business sector for years. For too long, people who have been called by God to ventures outside of the church have received the message that their jobs were somehow less spiritual. But, by teaching businessmen and women about how much God longs to be a part of their companies, Andy has started to see incredible miracles of provision, new ideas, and healing inside of businesses.

He has been using Communion in his ministry to the business world as well. He has taken Communion into the prisons. There, the inmates are taught on Communion as a tool for healing, and they then take Communion with whatever food and drink the prisons provide for them. Andy explains to the inmates that they don't have to have someone lay hands on them to be healed. God is healing, so when He is present, healings happen. Andy has seen countless miracles within the prisons. We never want to reduce Communion to something small. No matter what we are using to take Communion, the importance is remembering the fullness of what Jesus paid for and receiving that fullness into every area. And, as Andy says, "If it can happen in your body, it can happen in your business."

He told the story of one international business friend who had started to press in to see more of God in his business. He'd already had a string of miraculous encounters with God's provision. With these testimonies behind him, he launched a new business with two different sides to the company. One side was getting a lot of traction and growing, but the other side had not started to move. Andy joined his friend in praying for breakthrough, thanking God for the miracles they had already witnessed in this man's life. Andy explained, "I felt like we should take Communion, pray and bless the business, believing that Jesus had already paid for everything within his business."

They took Communion inside of the office, and Andy was dropped off at the train station to catch his flight back to the US. By the time Andy was walking through customs back in the States, he had received an email from his friend. As soon as he had dropped Andy off, the man had returned to work. Once he arrived, though, he discovered that the once-stagnant workplace had suddenly received at least ten requests for quotes from all over the world from huge international companies. They were in business! The owner was so blown away by the presence of the Lord that he couldn't work for the rest of the day.

The Lord wants to invade every area of your life. He is not only interested in being with you in Heaven; He wants Heaven to invade earth in your families, in your businesses, and in your communities. The Bible says that He knows "*the very hairs of your head*" (Luke 12:7). He knows what is in our hearts, and He cares about what we care about. Andy Mason shared another, more personal story of learning to trust in the goodness of God and learning to rest in His presence as a son.

> We received our tax return with a surprise terminal tax payment of $15,000. This was primarily from a gift received that previous year that we put entirely toward the purchase of our home. My initial reaction was a lot of anxiety. How would we make this work? We could scrape together the payment but how would we afford other cash flow requirements in the near future—school fees, medical insurance.... The more I thought, the greater I experienced anxiety and then guilt for not stewarding my finances well enough. I schemed about different cost-cutting measures and payment plans to make it work. But my anxiety was evident to my wife.
>
> The next morning, after spending some time in prayer, I sensed God highlighting Romans 4:16:

"...[inheriting] the promise is the outcome of faith and depends [entirely] on faith in order that it might be given as an act of grace (unmerited favor)" (AMPC). My anxiety was evidence that I was leaning on my own ability for what God had already given as a promise. Anxiety never leads to inheritance. Only peace and rest do. I needed to change!

Soon after, my wife walked up to me with a suggestion that she does with the kids: "Why don't you take a tissue and write out the lies you are believing, then tear it up before God." Great idea!

So, I did. Actually, after I told my Heaven in Business class my struggles, I got the whole class to do the same for the lies they were believing. We had Communion, remembering the promise of Christ and the full and final work of the cross. We then helped one another tear up the lies.

A short while later I got back to my office to find an email from my accountant asking me to call her. She had some questions around the gift. After hearing my answers, she stated that the gift was a personal gift, not business, and as such, not taxable income. That meant that our new terminal tax payment was... ZERO.

I am learning to trust a good God.

RELEASING IT TO OUR KIDS

Some people grow up feeling terrified of Communion. Not so much because of the "*eat my flesh and drink my blood*" part (see John 6:56), but more often because of what it says in First Corinthians 11:27, "*Therefore whoever eats the bread or drinks the cup of the Lord in an unworthy manner, shall be guilty of the body and the blood of the Lord*" (NASB). I was talking to a friend recently who said that when she was young, she would frantically search her memory for every sin she could have committed in the last month. She would confess anything and everything, thinking that if she missed something, she might die right there on the wooden pew. Every month held a renewed sense of terror as she reached for the bread and juice.

This is not how it's supposed to be. It's funny to talk about now that she's an adult, but experiencing the sacrament of Communion is not something that should terrify our children. Communion is a powerful way to encounter the Lord, and we get to invite them into that with expectation. Seth Dahl, co-author of *Win-Win Parenting*, led Bethel's Children's Ministry for seven years. He does a brilliant job of empowering children to have their own God encounters. Children do not have a junior Holy Spirit.[3] On the contrary, they often have an easier time connecting with the presence of the Lord because they don't have years of "stuff" to unlearn. When leaders come into our environment needing a prophetic word, we will often ask the kids to minister to them. Their purity, fearlessness and lack of religion seem to allow them to hear God's voice in a way that often leaves their audiences profoundly moved.

But God wants to use them to change the world just as much as He wants to use an adult. They have access to Him in the same way, and Communion can be a powerful tool for them to connect with the presence of God. But, often, it feels a bit intimidating to try to teach kids about something like Communion. Seth broke down how he does it, explaining that the most important things to focus on when teaching children anything are to wipe out fear, make it fun, and take our time.

Seth uses Hebrews to help give the kids a visualization of the New Covenant as he introduces Communion.

Therefore, brethren, since we have confidence to enter the holy place by the blood of Jesus, by a new and living way which He inaugurated for us through the veil, that is, His flesh, and since we have a great priest over the house of God, let us draw near with a sincere heart in full assurance of faith, having our hearts sprinkled clean from an evil conscience and our bodies washed with pure water (Hebrews 10:19-22 NASB).

The juice represents the blood of Jesus, he explains to the kids, and this blood gives us access into a place we were never able to go before. Before Jesus died, only a few very special people could go in to the presence of God. No one else could. So, when we drink the juice, we're remembering that we can go *boldly* before the presence of God. It's not just the high priest who can enter the presence of God—all of us can! Seth explains to the kids about the veil that was torn. The veil is like His flesh, so when we take Communion, we are saying, "Thank you, Jesus, that You have torn the veil and that you've washed us in your blood so that we can come into the presence of God." He encourages the kids to remember what Jesus gave us on the cross, remember what He did—our old, sinful man has passed away, His blood washed us as white as snow, and we are raised again as a new creation. We are now saints! We also remember that by His stripes we are healed. So we're not just remembering the moment Jesus died on the cross; we're remembering all that the cross did for us.

During this year's Tent Revival Camp, the nine- to twelve-year-olds ended their time at camp with Communion. The speaker taught the group of kids what Communion was and the power of it. He focused on offense and unforgiveness, and he explained to the group how devastating those things can be to our hearts. When he asked if anyone was carrying that in their hearts, several of the kids raised their hands. They were walked through the process of forgiveness as a group and then took Communion with God. As the meeting was coming to an end, the presence of God filled the camp. Relationships that had been noticeably strained during camp were mended, and kids began having encounters with the Lord. Amy Gagnon, the current Director of Bethel's Children's Ministry, explained, "That night, the Spirit of God broke out and several children walked into deep encounters with the Lord. They felt the physical weight of God in the room and upon them."

In Bethel Christian School, Communion is often introduced to the children in the springtime, around Easter. The teaching team begins the lesson by walking the kids through a beautiful explanation of sin. Each child draws a bull's-eye on a piece of paper while the teacher explains that sin isn't this shameful burden we need to bear; sin is simply missing the mark, and repentance is returning to right focus. The kids then have an opportunity to privately write on their bull's-eye the ways that they have "missed the mark." Tawny Novosad, one of our amazing teachers, explained to me that the sins the kids write down on their paper are often things that have been weighing heavily on their hearts. She makes sure to tell them that once the paper is folded up, it's between them and God. She won't look unless they want to share it with her.

THE POWER OF COMMUNION

With that paper in their hands, the kids move into a soaking time where Tawny invites them to see Jesus on the cross and ask Him to show them what carrying their sin felt like. It's a somber moment for the kids, as they encounter the effect that their sins had on Jesus. Even though there are often tears, for many of the kids it's a moment of encountering Jesus in an entirely new way.

With this new awareness, the kids walk from their classroom across campus to our Prayer Chapel, where they take Communion. It's a reverent time. She explains to them that we need the body and blood of Christ so that we don't have to carry that sin anymore. Once they take the Communion, thanking Jesus for all that He did on the cross, it's time for a dance party. Tawny puts on an old song called, "Stomp on the Devil's Head," the kids take their pieces of paper—the ways that they've been missing the mark—and they choose a prophetic act. They either shred the paper up or crumple it in their hands, and then they dance on top it. They celebrate the fact that Jesus paid for their sins so that they could be children of righteousness. They stomp on the sin that was weighing them down. Then they cheer and dance together, celebrating their new reality.

LET IT OUT

Many years ago, we had a strange experience where a roadrunner kept coming to our prayer meetings. For months, this bird would show up outside of the building when we would gather to worship. We had no idea what was going on, but it felt significant. One night, the bird snuck in the building while one of our custodial team was cleaning. Every time the custodian would stop working to put on some worship music, the bird would stop and watch. Every time the young man would move, the bird would follow him. After a while of this, a door opened from another room and spooked the bird. It ran down the hallway into the plate-glass window and died. The whole story was too strange, so Bill went to the Lord and just asked Him what was going on with this bird. Very clearly, he heard, "What I'm bringing into the House, had better have a way of being released from the House or it will die in the House."[4]

The Spirit of God lives inside every believer and will never leave. But we have the honor of stewarding His presence. God has given the gift of His body and blood to His Church. But I want to encourage you to release

the power of Communion from the four walls of the church and into your family, your business, your community, etc. There is no area of your life that Communion with God cannot improve. Take these testimonies as your own. The Bible says that *"the testimony of Jesus is the spirit of prophesy"* (Rev. 19:10). Whatever God has done before, He wants to do again. Grab ahold of them. Let your faith rise. Align yourself with the resurrected Christ. And witness the wonder-working power of Jesus.

NOTES

1. Beni Johnson, *The Happy Intercessor* (Shippensburg, PA: Destiny Image Publishers, Inc., 2009).

2. *Blue Letter Bible*, s.v. "kataggello," https://www. blueletterbible.org/lang/lexicon/lexicon .cfm?t=kjv&strongs=g2605.

3. This saying was coined by Kathie and David Walters and often quoted by others.

4. Bill Johnson, Bethel Church message, https://www .youtube.com/watch?v=kw1yOKov5GE.

Chapter 7

THE POSTURE OF OUR HEARTS

Jesus never requires perfection in order to come to Him. That is the scandal of His saving grace. We don't need to be anxious about taking Communion, searching for any potential hidden sin. Fear is never productive; it just gets in the way of love's transforming power. However, when we participate in the body and blood of Christ, we do want to posture our hearts in an intentional way. This intentionality not only brings the respect and honor due to the sacrament, but it also helps us to create the space in our hearts for the Spirit of God to move and transform us through Communion.

WITH SOBERNESS

Often, when we focus so much on what divides us, we can miss out on honoring some valuable aspects of different Christian traditions. Even though I love our free-flowing worship, there is something so beautiful about a formal liturgy. Similarly, I think we can learn from the way the Catholic Church honors Communion, teaching the children what it means and making a special event of their first occasion. When we participate in Communion, it is important for there to be a sense of soberness. I don't mean *somber*, as in "gloomy or depressing." Far from it. But there needs to be a sense of gravity about what we are getting to participate in.

We have such a good Father, who is so incredibly full of grace, but I would never want to lose sight of His holiness or His awesome power. On the one hand, we have Jesus, inviting the little children to come to Him. And, on the other, we have Jesus, returning to earth with eyes that flame like fire. It's not either/or; it's both/and. When we participate in the body and blood of Jesus Christ, sober reverence is a healthy and appropriate reaction.

The power of Communion—sometimes overlooked by Christians—has not been missed by the occult. One of our dear friends and former leaders at Bethel, Sue Manwaring, grew up with an understanding of the power of Communion. But it was taught to her by her family members who were involved in extreme witchcraft. She explained that as a part of the satanic rituals, they would mimic Christian rituals. So, they took Communion, but instead of the blood and body of Christ, it involved horrific abuse. She was led through the Christian salvation prayer at an early age, but even that was twisted. The purpose of her salvation, according to her abusers, was not so that Sue could experience life with Christ, but so that they could prove to her that Jesus wouldn't rescue her. They filled her mind with lies, thinking they could prove to her that Jesus did not want her.

"Whilst the Church does Communion thanking Jesus for the cross, we did Communion to the devil," Sue explained. "Doing Communion to Jesus was such a huge issue that I was never supposed to do it. It went against everything I was being raised in. Communion [with Jesus] was like the ultimate betrayal." Years later, when she was free from her abusers, happily married, and walking with the Lord, she was walking through healing from her traumatic past with a counselor at Bethel.

During one session, after he had heard more of her story, the counselor asked her how she felt about taking Communion. "Honestly, I did not think it would be an issue at all...so we went ahead with Communion and, as I took a small piece of bread, my whole being reacted." Thrown into traumatic flashbacks of the "Communion" of her childhood, Sue described taking the juice as "searing heat and pain...I can still remember today what it felt like—indescribable pain and awfulness in celebrating Jesus' body and blood shed for me."

For weeks, she tried taking Communion during every session with the counselor as they worked through the healing of her childhood. Eventually, they put a pause on trying to involve Communion. The traumatic flashbacks were actually making it harder to receive breakthrough with the counseling. Sue was open with the leadership about her inability to take Communion, and we knew that she was actively pursuing healing. But, every month, when the plates of bread and cups of juice would be passed around, Sue would excuse herself and go to the restroom.

One Sunday, as Communion started, she heard the Lord say, "It's today." Instead of running away, she walked forward to a pastor who knew her story. He looked at her and asked, "Is today the day?" She nodded her head, but internally felt terrified of the pain and potential embarrassment that might occur if she couldn't take it. Mustering all of her courage, she took the bread and then drank the juice. And there was no pain. She was free. "Finally, I had broken that power over me and beaten the enemy. Communion should never be taken lightly. It was one of the hardest and longest periods of my life, trying to get healing and breakthrough in this area." Sue's story is one of radical freedom and transformation. But it also points to the very real power of Communion, a time when we get to remember the gravity of what has been done for us on the cross. We get to participate in the blood and body of Christ with as much reverence and honor as that reality demands.

WITH THANKFULNESS

Thankfulness is showing appreciation. The Bible tells us to "*Rejoice always; pray without ceasing; in everything*

give thanks; for this is God's will for you in Christ Jesus" (1Thess. 5:16-18 NASB). I often hear people yearning to know God's will for their lives, but it says it right here. Stay thankful. Stay connected to God. When the Bible tells us to be thankful no matter the circumstance, it is not expecting us to create an emotion out of thin air. Gratitude is a response. There has to be a previous action or reality. When we take Communion, we are responding to all that the Lord has done and continues to do for us. Keeping our hearts postured toward the Lord in gratitude is one of the biggest keys to success we find throughout the Bible.

Hebrews 13:15 encourages us to *"continually offer up a sacrifice of praise to God"* (NASB). We've all been in the midst of experiences where the phrase *"sacrifice of praise"* feels very real. When you're exhausted or hurting, sometimes worship and expressing gratitude is the last thing you want to do. But look at the Samaritan leper. Ten leprous men were healed by Jesus, but only one of them fell down to give Him thanks. Jesus wasn't in need of gratitude, but He knew that it would do something for the man. Jesus asked about the other nine men who hadn't returned, and then He told the Samaritan, *"Stand up and go; your faith has made you well"* (Luke 17:19 NASB). The man was already healed. But that word *"well"* is that Hebrew word *sozo* again. His body had been healed, but there was something about his expression of gratitude that made him whole.

Psalm 50 says that *"He who offers a sacrifice of thanksgiving honors Me; And to him who orders his way aright I shall show the salvation of God"* (Ps. 50:23 NASB). This is such a powerful verse. We have been made *"a royal priesthood"* (1 Pet. 2:9). As believers under the New Covenant, we now have the privilege of ministering to the Lord. When we offer up a *"sacrifice of praise,"* we are bringing honor to God. Focusing our hearts on gratitude brings Him glory, which alone is enough. But the Bible goes on to explain that gratitude also reorients us correctly, inviting the *"salvation of God"* into our lives. That word "salvation" is the Hebrew word *yesha*, which means "rescue and safety," but it also means "deliverance, prosperity, and victory."[1] The psalmist said to *"enter His gates with thanksgiving and His courts with praise"* (Ps. 100:4 NASB). When we come to the Lord with thankfulness, we have access to His presence and His covering. We get to participate in His victory.

Our friends, Michael and Jessica Koulianos, shared an amazing testimony with me about Jessica's maternal grandfather, Roy Harthern. In the late 1990s, Roy was dying of kidney cancer. He had spent his life pastoring a large Assembly of God church, but he got sick and was not getting better. As the family traveled to his bedside to say goodbye to their grandfather, he was carrying a mere 80 pounds on his 6'1" frame. A pastor friend, who was a great Bible teacher, contacted the family and told them that Roy needed to start taking Communion every day. The pastor connected with Roy and began to teach him about the power of the sacrament. Despite his condition, Roy began to align himself daily with the body and blood of Christ through Communion.

One night, shortly after, Roy had an encounter with the Lord. Jesus entered his room and told Roy that He was going to heal his body. That night, Roy received two brand-new kidneys. Not only was the terminal cancer completely gone from his body, but the tests revealed that Roy suddenly had the kidneys of a much younger man. The doctor, a staunch atheist, didn't know how to comprehend what had happened to his dying patient. He could find no medical explanation for the sudden changes in Roy's body. He ended up admitting, "There has to be a God!" Even though he had refused God's existence, he suddenly saw the lack of evidence on the side of atheism. This supernatural, creative miracle pushed the doctor right out of his unbelief. Roy left that hospital and lived for another 20 years, sharing his testimony of God's healing and the power of Communion.

I can't hear that story without feeling overwhelmed with gratitude. Even if you don't have a personal story like this, you do have a God like this. Each of our lives testifies of His goodness and faithfulness. We just need to cultivate the awareness. When we take Communion, we get to collect those stones of remembrance of His goodness and create a monument of thankfulness in our hearts. The heart of praise allows us to draw near to Him, and that is the entire focus of Communion.

WITH CELEBRATION

I love the story of the first miracle that Jesus did. I love that Mary pulled Jesus' public ministry into the limelight before it was time. And I love that Jesus created wine for a party. Jesus loves celebration. The dictionary defines "celebration" as "the action of marking one's pleasure at an important event or occasion by engaging in enjoyable, typically social, activity."[2] We can celebrate alone, of course, but more often a celebration is an experience we want to share with the people we love. When we take Communion, it is our chance to celebrate with our brothers and sisters in Christ. Jesus has changed our lives, and that deserves a party. After all, what's a celebration without friends? A lot of this book has centered around taking Communion individually, or maybe family members taking it together. But there is something very special about corporate Communion—partaking of the body and blood of Christ with the vibrant, diverse Body of Christ. Communion is a vertical realigning of ourselves with Christ, but it is also a horizontal realigning: We are the Body of Christ.

Damaris Stevens has been running Communion at Bethel with her family since 2009. Several years ago, as she was orchestrating the passing of the bread and juice cups, she was feeling discouraged. The church was growing rapidly, but her volunteers hadn't grown at the same speed, so her family was working hard. As she was standing in the back of the sanctuary, pouring her heart out to the Lord, she heard Him say, "You're thinking about the work and not thinking about the *joy* in the work." She stopped and, looking around, saw the packed sanctuary in a different light. Literally. "All of a sudden, it felt like the whole room changed to a deeper color as I looked around at people taking Communion. They glowed! Not like a light, but more like their colors became vivid. Like, as they took Communion, they went from analog to high definition." Immediately, her heart turned from being focused on the work to being aware of the powerful moment in the Spirit that she was getting to facilitate.

God loves unity. It was His idea. This is why examining our hearts is such an important part of Communion. Not because we have to prove to God that we're worthy of His blood and body. We already know that's impossible. We examine our hearts because it's a time of reunion, both with the Spirit of God and with our fellow believers. In corporate Communion, we get to stand with others and confess that He took a burden from our shoulders that we could never carry. Experiencing that radical grace means that we now get to access and release that grace to others. We get to offer forgiveness to others, cleansing our hearts from the detrimental effects of bitterness and unforgiveness.

The individual relationship with God is crucial to our lives and foundational to our beliefs. We must have that time in the secret place. But the Lord also loves it when we gather, united, in His name. He promises that "*where two or three have gathered together in My name, I am there in their midst*" (Matt. 18:20 NASB). And, as we can see from His very first miracle, Jesus loves a good party, and He doesn't want the supplies to run out! Bethel has grown rapidly since Damaris started providing Communion, and that has meant creating both additional Sunday service times and additional locations. Presently, there are six services happening every Sunday morning and nine services each weekend. Twice when a service had been added to a Sunday morning, Damaris found that she had greatly underestimated the amount of the elements that would be needed. "I found myself praying that there would be enough for those last services, knowing full well there wasn't anywhere near enough."

On both occasions, though, something strange happened. Trays of bread and juice would go out to the congregation to be passed along the rows of people, like they were normally. But instead of returning almost empty, trays began to return to her full, as if they hadn't been touched. "Usually, there is only a little bit of bread and a just a few juices left, if any. But for every service on these two occasions, it was like the bread and juice had been replaced every time someone picked up an element. It felt like a little miracle just for our team to show us that God really cared about what we were doing for the church."

Communion is a time of celebration. Like eating the wedding cake and toasting with champagne after the vows have been exchanged, Communion commemorates the covenant that has been made between our Creator and ourselves. This celebration also solidifies and reminds us of the union that we have with those around us. Jesus loves His Church. He is coming back for a strong, healthy, and united Bride.

YOU ARE THE LIGHT OF THE WORLD

It's all about Him. Everything changes when we align ourselves with God. As Bill says, "The Holy Spirit wants to reveal Himself *to* you so that He can reveal Himself *through* you." We are citizens of Heaven, but we have an assignment to fulfill on earth—that is releasing the reality of Heaven into every situation, every relationship, and every corner of the earth. But how can we do that? Not through our own strength, surely. Scripture says that "*we have the mind of Christ*" (1Cor. 2:16). It says that we have died and have been raised with Jesus (see Rom. 6:4). It says that our old man has gone and we are a new creation (see 2 Cor. 5:17) and that Christ lives within us (see Gal. 2:20). The Bible is 100% true, so if I'm not experiencing those statements all of the time, then there must be a reality that is greater and *truer* than the one that I am experiencing.

That we would need reminding of this greater reality comes as no surprise to the Lord. It's like He sat us all down at that table with the disciples in that upper room and said, "Listen, I know. I know some days are going to be hard. I know there are going to be moments when it feels like the reality of Heaven is far away. Your child is sick or you lost your job or your best friend died or you did that thing you swore you would stop doing. I know. I'm leaving you something—My body and My blood— to remind you who you are and where your true home is. I'm leaving you this reminder of My salvation, My healing, the comfort of My presence, and My victorious return. Take it. Remember me. Be everything I created you to be so that My Kingdom can invade every single one of those situations, and the world can know a good, good Father."

Human nature is constantly attempting to create rules outside of a relationship. Communion is not a magic pill, and God is not a vending machine. He does not want us to eat a wafer and drink some grape juice every day so that He will grant our wishes. Communion is about lining ourselves up with Him—spirit, soul, and body. It is a chance for us to remember the debt of sin that hung around our necks—too big for us to ever repay on our own—and the way that our Jesus took that debt with Him to the cross so that you and I could "*have life, and have it abundantly*" (John 10:10 NASB). It's a chance for us to come—in all humility and honor—into the presence of the Lord, to praise His name for all that He has done, and to celebrate in union with other believers. Take this tool, given to us by Jesus Himself, and use it frequently. You will not remain the same. That is His promise.

NOTES

1. *Blue Letter Bible,* s.v. "yesha," https://www
    .blueletterbible.org/lang/lexicon/lexicon
    .cfm?Strongs=H3468&t=NASB

2. Google Dictionary

Chapter 8

DEVELOPING
THE HABIT

BILL JOHNSON

We are taught in the Scriptures that in taking Communion we are *proclaiming the Lord's death until He comes* (see 1 Cor. 11:26). I like to picture *proclaiming* as a bold and confident shout! We are declaring in fullness the redemptive work of Jesus found in the Gospel. Every time we take the bread and the wine/juice in remembrance, it is a prophetic proclamation of what has already happened, as well as what is yet to come. Consider this, Communion declares that Jesus died for us and is returning for us.

When people surrender their life to Jesus, they are born again. In other words, they're saved. We know this teaching from God's Word. But then the Bible also says, "*Work out your own salvation with fear and trembling*" (Phil. 2:12). The implication is that I am also *being saved*. This doesn't deny what happened to me when I received Christ. It just emphasizes the daily ongoing process of personal transformation. So, not only were you once saved, but you are also being saved right now. The crowning touch to this glorious truth of our salvation comes when we die to meet Him or He returns to take us to Heaven. In this coming event, we find that we *will be* saved. Our salvation will then be complete. Participating in Communion is a wonderful privilege that declares what I call *the bookends of our salvation* in that it addresses the past and the future. Sharing in the broken body and the shed blood of Jesus helps us with the present.

THE IMPORTANCE OF THANKFULNESS

The most complete passage on the rite of Communion in the Bible is found in First Corinthians 11. In it, Paul unwraps the insight given to him through an encounter with Jesus Himself. In verses 23 and 24, he says, *"For I received from the Lord that which I also delivered to you: that the Lord Jesus on the same night in which He was betrayed took bread; and when He had given thanks, He broke it and said, 'Take, eat.'"* Please picture something powerful—the very night that Jesus was betrayed, He gave thanks. In the midst of the ultimate betrayal, He gave an offering of thanksgiving. He didn't just tell us to praise Him in hard times; He gave us the ultimate example to follow. In betrayal, He gave thanks.

Thankfulness is one of the most vital attributes within the reach of every person alive. If I could prayerfully lay hands on people and impart a thankful heart, without question, I would. And I would make that the single greatest focus of my life. An impartation of thankfulness would have the greatest impact on the hearts and minds of people. It would literally change the world as we know it. Thankful people attract breakthrough.

Following the major sporting events like the Super Bowl, World Series, World Cup, and the like, it has become common to see athletes thank God for enabling them to win. I love to see them boast in God and testify of Him every chance they get. But let's be honest, it's not that challenging to give thanks when you've won. The real prize is when we give Him thanks in the middle of something difficult or wrong. That's where the pearl is formed, so to speak. Pearls are formed through irritation. Whenever we give thanks in the middle of hard things, we are presenting something to Him that is priceless. Jesus did it at His darkest moment—betrayal.

THE IMPORTANCE OF REMEMBRANCE

In verse 24, Jesus said of the bread, *"'Take, eat; this is my body which is broken for you.'"* Please listen to what He said. He said, *"This is my body...."* There is an invitation into a kind of reverence with this statement. *"...which is broken for you, do this in remembrance of Me."* Verse 25 continues: *"In the same manner He also took the cup after supper, saying, 'This cup is the new covenant in My blood. This do, as often as you drink it, in remembrance of Me.'"*

It's just like the Lord to give us things to do that position us to remember Him. Making this a ritual or tradition that has lost its meaning is so unnecessary. In our hearts, we all have the intention of serving the Lord fully and with complete abandonment. But if you're like me, you probably sometimes go for hours in a day without thinking of Him. We're living from His blessing, from His commission, but there are times in the day that we aren't abiding in that face-to-face privilege that we have with God. We are working faithfully, playing with the kids or taking care of our daily business. With no condemnation, we can all admit that life gets busy. But in His kindness, the Lord gives us tools that help us to bring Him back into our minds.

Pausing to remember is a principle established throughout Scripture. In the Old Testament, Israel miraculously crossed a river on dry ground. Once they did, they were instructed to put a pile of stones on the same side of the river they crossed over to. This way every time they passed the place where the miraculous had occurred, the stones would trigger the memory. The goodness of the Lord was brought back to mind. (See Joshua 4:1-24.) The devil wants to control your memories. He wants to influence how you think about your past. He wants to influence your perspective on the reality that's going on around you. And he does so by keeping you focused on the things that were disappointing, or the areas of past failures, or where you were wronged. The Lord, on the other hand, constantly invites you to return to a redemptive focus where you concern yourself with what God is saying and what God is doing.

PARTAKING WORTHILY

Paul gives us a somber warning in verse 27: *"Whoever eats the bread or drinks the cup of the Lord in an unworthy manner, shall be guilty of the body and the blood of the Lord"* (NASB). This is an interesting part of Communion. Communion hurts you if you're not saved but advances you if you are. The anointing of God doesn't always have the same effect on people. The Presence that brings you peace will sometimes irritate others.

Paul admonishes, *"Let a man examine himself, so let him eat of the bread and drink of the cup"* (1 Cor. 11:28). Verse 29 is key for us. *"For he who eats and drinks in an unworthy manner, eats and drinks judgment to himself not discerning the Lord's body."* Paul is defining what it looks like to eat and to drink in an unworthy manner. None of us are clean enough on our own to be worthy to participate in Communion. Jesus is the One whose blood makes us clean enough to celebrate the broken body and blood of Jesus. It is His provision for us. But, in this context, Paul is explaining that judgment has come through a lack of discerning the body.

When Jesus broke the bread, He said, *"This is my body"* (1 Cor. 11:24). And Paul said people eat judgment to themselves by not discerning the body correctly. Every time you take Communion and are holding the bread in your hand, you hold something that has value, deserves recognition and can carry judgment. When we hold the bread of Communion, we recognize that it is a divine moment. The body in this context is most likely referring to the bread we hold in our hands. But there is also reason to think He is referring to the Body of Christ, which is the people of God. Both perspectives have merit and are easy to apply in this setting. Placing correct value on the bread I hold, believing it is the body of Jesus, has tremendous impact on the effect of that act. But it could also be said that giving proper esteem to the people of God as the Body of Christ also has value in this context. The point is, don't reduce this to a mindless ritual. Think, pray, and give thanks.

Paul goes on to say, "For this reason, many are weak and sick, and many sleep or have died" (see verse 30). He is saying there are people in the Body of Christ who will go to Heaven, but because they did not realize the meaning of what was in their hands, they reduced Communion to a religious ritual. Without realizing it, they removed the tool that God had put in their life to bring divine health. And for that reason, many are weak or sick, and some have even died. Yet, presumably, week after week, month after month, the miracle was in their hand. But a wrong perspective cancels out the power of that moment. One book calls this "the meal that heals."[1] Well said.

HEALING IN COMMUNION

Isaiah 53, the prophetic passage on healing, reads, *"Surely He has borne our griefs..."* (verse 4). The literal word for "griefs" is *sicknesses*. In this passage, Isaiah is, in fact, saying, *"Surely He has borne our [sicknesses]. He carried our pains. Yet we esteemed him stricken, smitten by God and afflicted."* When Jesus died on the cross, the Scripture says, "He became sin." (See 2 Cor. 5:21.) And when He became sin and died in our place, the Father's anger and wrath were poured out on Him as He became the very thing that was working to destroy us. He took my place and bore what I deserved. Jesus asked the Father, "Why did you turn your face from me? Why did you forsake me?" (See Matthew 27:46 and Psalm 22:1.) The Father forsook Him because Jesus became sin. He poured out His wrath upon His own Son, who had become what was destroying mankind.

The movie, *The Passion of the Christ*, is probably the clearest pictorial description of the sufferings of Christ available at this moment. Isaiah 53:5 records, *"He was wounded for our transgressions, He was bruised for our iniquities; the chastisement for our peace was upon Him, and by His stripes we are healed."* When the Scripture is talking about stripes, it is talking about His physical beating. They beat Jesus with a rod, and of course He wore the crown of thorns, but those things were minor compared to being whipped with metal shards tied onto leather straps.

The tradition of the day was to use the whip in cases like this and give specifically 39 lashes. That number was so severe, it actually opened up their flesh to their internal organs. The understanding was that 40 lashes would kill a man, so they would take him to the edge of death instead. When we say that *"by His stripes we are healed,"* we're talking about the beating that He endured. We're talking about the moment when Jesus made a payment for our health and our healing. This part of His suffering was not to make it possible for us to go to Heaven. This one, in many ways, is for Heaven to come to earth in us. His blood paid the price to get you to Heaven. But His stripes were actually a payment for our pain, suffering and sicknesses here on earth.

Everybody knows you get a new body in Heaven. There's no sickness there, there's no weeping there, there's no pain, no conflict, no confusion. In Heaven, everything is wonderful. So, it's important to see that this part of His provision is for now. *"By His stripes we are healed"* (Is. 53:5). Peter quoted the passage from Isaiah in this way: *"by whose stripes you were healed"* (1 Pet. 2:24). Notice it is past tense. It has already been accomplished on our behalf.

The body of the broken Savior made a full and complete payment, not only for my healing, but for health—spirit, soul, and body. This is the provision of the Lord. And that's its purpose. Remembering Jesus' broken body in Communion is not just a nice sentimental moment when we give thanks that He died and we get to go to Heaven. It is all that, but a million times more. It's a divine moment.

Let's say somebody gives you a car. They've gone down to the dealership and paid in cash, and they say, "Just go on down there, give them this card, and they'll give you the car. Everything has been paid for—the taxes are paid, the tank is full of gas and I've covered insurance for the first five years. Go, get your car!" It would be foolish for you to go down there and insist on paying for the car again. Yet many people are trying to pay for their healing that's already been purchased. It's a gift that we all qualify for.

Then how is it that Jesus could heal people during His earthly ministry before He had borne stripes on His body? I look at it like when we went grocery shopping with our whole family when the children were small.

The key to sane shopping with young children is the ice cream aisle. We strategically went down the ice cream aisle first and got an ice cream for each of the kids before we did any of our shopping. It was amazing how angelic they were with an ice cream cone in their hands. We hadn't paid for that ice cream yet, but neither had we left the store. We would put the wrapper in the cart so the cashier could scan it with the rest of the groceries. We paid for what was already consumed before we left the store. And when Jesus died, He paid for everything that had already been consumed *before He left the store*.

Communion Means War

Beni teaches that Communion is a weapon of war, and I really believe that. This meal is not only an act of celebration but also a military tool of battle. We may not feel like we are engaging in war, but there are many things that we do—celebrating His kindness and His goodness, delighting in His presence, and giving praise—that all have a military effect on the demonic realm. Psalm 68:1 says, *"Let God arise, let His enemies be scattered"* (NASB). When we exalt the Lord, there is an effect on the realms of darkness.

The Lord has given us basically four different weapons for spiritual warfare: the blood of Jesus (Communion), the Word of God, the name of Jesus and praise. Those are the four basic weapons that we believers use in our life that defeats and overcomes the assaults that the enemy brings against us. None of them are focused on the devil. All of them are focused on the provision of the Lord, and the Person of the Lord Jesus Christ.

As a church, we're on a journey to learn how to access all that God has purchased for us. The blood of Jesus is the legal basis for all victory. The cross of Jesus was so thorough in its victory that everything you will ever need throughout eternity was purchased at this one event. There's no other event in history that was so all-inclusive. A hundred billion years from now we will still be feeding off of what was provided for in the sacrifice of this unblemished Lamb.

COMMUNION AND PRAYER FOR FAMILY

I try to take Communion every day. While I'm not always successful, Beni and I have made this a regular part of our daily life, even when traveling. When we do

this in our corporate gatherings, it looks a bit different in that it takes a few minutes of our service. But when I'm alone, or with Beni, we like to take a bit more time than is reasonable in our corporate Communion time on a Sunday morning.

Beni and I often take Communion together, but a couple of years ago, I got too sick to even take Communion. Beni would sit by my bed and take it for me. We would just sit there together and give thanks to God for His goodness. She would take Communion, we'd hold hands, and we'd pray. We would just thank the Lord for His provision, for healing, for divine health. Our approach to life is to see in completion what Christ had accomplished for us and make the decree, By His stripes I was healed. (See 1 Peter 2:24.)

It's important to remind ourselves as we take Communion that it is because of the sacrifice of the Lamb of God that we are alive, that we are forgiven, that we have hope. I pray this reality over each individual in my family. I pray over Eric and Candace, over Kennedy and Selah. I pray for each of them. I pray for the journey that they're on that God would pour out great wisdom and

grace upon them, that He'd fill them with prosperity of spirit, soul and body.

I pray for Brian and Jenn, and I pray for Haley, Téa, Braden, and Moses. I plead the blood of Jesus over every family member. I pray for Gabe and Leah and for their children Judah, Diego, Bella and Cruz. And I pray that God would give each one of my family members a heart to know Him (see Jer. 24). I pray that God would deepen their encounters with Him. I pray that He would visit them in the night and visit them in the day. In the Old Testament, one lamb was sacrificed for the entire household. They didn't sacrifice lambs for each individual. They sacrificed one per household. God designed families to be saved together. It was His idea to have entire family lines dedicated to serving the Lord. In this time of prayer for each family member, I confess and declare, *"As for me and my house, we will serve the Lord"* (Josh. 24:15).

The promise of household salvation carries over into the New Testament. The jailer was saved and soon after his encounter, his entire household was converted (see Acts 16:31-34). That is the standard of the Lord. Don't settle for any other. Don't be impressed with the sin your loved one may be involved in; be impressed with the power of the blood of Jesus.

A wonderful testimony illustrates the power of prayer for a loved one during Communion. We have friends in another state whose son a number of years ago was in extreme rebellion. The things that he would do right in front of his mother's face were just terrifying. One Sunday, his mother was taking Communion in church, and she thought she should plead the blood of Jesus over her son. She just began to pray, declaring that the blood of Jesus sets him free. About two hours after she got home from church, he called in absolute full repentance for his lifestyle of rebellion. This is it, one lamb per household.

COMMUNION AND PRAYER FOR OTHERS

I begin Communion by praying over my family members, but then I move outward. Like a pebble dropped into water, my prayers ripple outward. I begin to pray for Kris and Kathy and some of the other ones that are so close to me. I begin to pray for absolute blessing over their families, for the fulfillment of dreams in their lives. After that, I move to three other individuals whom I won't mention by name. Three leaders in the body of Christ have worked very hard to oppose what is happening here at Bethel. They have attacked me personally by name in their meetings and books. It has become common for them to attack this church body and our friends in the ministry. Their efforts are very zealous in their attempt to destroy what's happening here.

So I include them in my time with the Lord. When I pray for them, I make sure not to pray at them. I never accuse another person before the Lord. The Bible warns us of the foolishness of accusing a servant to his master. They're not my servant; I have no authority over them. Instead, I hold the blood of Jesus out, and I say, "Lord, I ask that You would bless the lives of these men. I ask that You would fulfill their dreams, that they would see their families in total health, that they would see their whole family line serve the Lord. I ask that they would live a long life, celebrating your kindness and your goodness. That You'd increase the encounters in their life. That they'd so prosper." I pray for each of them by name. And I take this moment to be a friend who prays for those who—for whatever reason—have decided to be enemies.

Even if they're misinformed, they're displaying their zeal in serving the Lord, and I honor that.

From there I move on to other friends and ministries, some of whom are much different in their approach to God and life. Supporting them in prayer is a great privilege, and a wonderful reminder that we need the whole body of Christ. None of us have it all. We need each other.

SCARING THE ENEMY

I believe in the power of Communion so much that I love to make confession over my family of how the blood of Jesus sets us free. This confession absolutely terrifies parts of darkness. I know from personal experience that it's the one thing of which they are absolutely terrified. They know that the blood of Jesus is the dividing line that separates someone the demonic can control from someone they can't touch.

I love to hold this before the Lord and pray for the people around me. I just plead the blood of Jesus over their lives. I want to encourage you to pick up a similar habit. It's not just grape juice that we're drinking. I pray that each of us would fully realize the effect of what we're doing during Communion. I believe that the Lord is going to release unusual miracles of healing in the taking of the bread. He is going to release unusual miracles of deliverance to people and family members, who are maybe a thousand miles away or more by our taking the juice (representing the blood) and pleading the blood of Jesus over their lives.

Prayer while partaking of Communion is possibly one of the most underrated prayers that we could ever pray. Communion is not a magic formula. It's us, being convinced that the blood of Jesus sets free. And that expression of faith puts us into a position to influence the destinies of our families, the people around us and the entire world.

NOTES

1. Perry Stone, *The Meal That Heals: Enjoying Intimate, Daily Communion with God* (Lake Mary: Charisma House, 2008).

LET'S TAKE COMMUNION TOGETHER

Read this aloud with me:

*W*hen evening came, Jesus was reclining at the table with the twelve disciples. And as they were eating, He said, "I assure you and most solemnly say to you that one of you will betray Me." Being deeply grieved and extremely distressed, each one of them began to say to Him, "Surely not I, Lord?" Jesus answered, "He who has dipped his *hand in the bowl with Me [as a pretense of friend-ship] will betray Me. The Son of Man is to go [to the cross], just as it is written [in Scripture] of Him; but woe (judgment is coming) to that man by whom the Son of Man is betrayed! It would have been good for that man if he had never been born." And Judas, the betrayer, said, "Surely it is not I, Rabbi?" Jesus said to him, "You have said it yourself."*

Now as they were eating Jesus took bread, and after blessing it, He broke it and gave it to the disciples, and said, "Take, eat; this is My body" (Matthew 26:20-26 AMP).

The only requirement for you to take Communion is that you know Jesus Christ as your personal Savior. If that is not the case, you can confess your sins and invite Him to be the Lord of your life right now. There's no better moment than this one to step into His freedom and grace.

We do want to examine our hearts, though, before we take this together. Jesus came as our example. Everything that Jesus did here on earth was an example for us to model in our daily lives. In these verses that we just read, we see a stunning example of the purity of His heart. As soon as Jesus talks about the impending betrayal, He turns around and praises God. God, help us to do the same.

Being rejected or betrayed has been a part of all of our lives. So, just take a moment right now and ask yourself a few questions. Is there anyone that you need to forgive? Is there anyone whom you have been unkind to? Ask God to forgive you, and commit to Him that you will go and make things right as soon as this is done.

If there is any bitterness or unforgiveness inside of you, you want to give that to Him. It's of no use to you; it will destroy you. Forgive anyone you need to forgive, and make it right with God right now.

Hold the bread in your hands.

This bread represents Jesus and His broken body. It represents our healing. Do you need healing in your body? Do you need emotional freedom? Is your spirit crushed and you need Jesus' healing touch? If you need a miracle, put your hand on your heart. Let this prophetic word from Isaiah sink into your spirit:

But He was wounded for our transgressions,

He was crushed for our wickedness [our sin, our injustice, our wrongdoing];

The punishment [required] for our well-being fell on Him,

And by His stripes (wounds) we are healed

(Isaiah 53:5 AMP).

We *are* healed. This is a prophetic depiction of all that Jesus would accomplish—peace, well-being, and healing.

You are healed.

I'm going to declare this over you:

Your body, your soul, and your spirit will be well in the name of Jesus. You will walk in well-being. He died for you. He died for me. Jesus, come. Thank You for your broken body. Right here, there are people who need Your healing presence, Jesus. I declare healing into you by the power of Jesus. That you would walk in total well-being. Thank You, Jesus, that You are no respecter of persons. Everyone can come to the table. Thank You, Jesus, that You are here.

Let's take the bread together.

Now, read this aloud with me:

And when He had taken a cup and given thanks, He gave it to them, saying, "Drink from it, all of you; for this is My blood of the [new and better] covenant, which [ratifies the agreement and] is being poured out for many [as a substitutionary atonement] for the forgiveness of sins (Mathew 26:27-28 AMP).

Take the cup in your hands.

This cup represents the blood of Jesus, our salvation. Jesus' blood changed everything for each one of us. Forever. When that stone was rolled away, He rose in victory. We get to participate in that victory and live forever under the New Covenant. You and I are able to go boldly before the throne of Heaven. And we have a Savior who intercedes on our behalf. You will never be alone. You will never be found unworthy of His love.

By His blood, we have been saved. We are saved, healed, and delivered.

Bill and I like to name each of our family members at this point. Join me, if you wish, in naming your loved ones out loud. Cover each one of them in the blood of Jesus. You can do the same with your nation, or whatever is sitting on your heart right now.

We are reminding ourselves that it was His blood that set us free.

Let's take the cup together, and let's celebrate today all that He did for us.

COMMUNION

ABOUT THE
AUTHOR

Beni and her husband, Bill Johnson, are the Senior Pastors of Bethel Church. Beni has a call to intercession that is an integral part of the Bethel Church mission. She was pivotal in the development of Bethel's Prayer House as well as the intercession team. Beni also carries a call to see the church become healthy and whole in their bodies, souls, and spirits. Her heart is to see the people of God live lives that are healthy and free and see them pave the way to bringing health back to the world as God intended. Her passion for people, health, and intercession have all helped to bring the much-needed breakthrough in Bethel's ministry. Beni's vision is to see the people of God live lives filled with joyful prayer, intercession, and complete wellness.